The Adaptive School

Developing and Facilitating

Collaborative Groups

Developed
by

Robert Garmston and Bruce Wellman

Selected illustrations by Michael Buckley

Fifth Edition

Printed in Canada

About the Authors

Robert J. Garmston consults with schools and professional organizations and conducts workshops for educators and educational agencies throughout North America and in Africa, Asia, Australia, Europe and the Middle East. In addition to working with educational clients, he has served police academies, the World Health Organization and the United States Air Force. Dr. Garmston is Professor Emeritus of Educational Administration at California State University, Sacramento, and Executive Director of Facilitation Associates, a consulting firm specializing in leadership, learning, and personal and organizational development. Formerly a classroom teacher, principal, director of instruction and superintendent, Dr. Garmston is co-developer of the Cognitive Coaching model with Dr. Arthur Costa. He lives near Sacramento, California with his wife Sue, and near to his five adult children, and five grandchildren, each of whom, of course, is bright and cute.

Bruce Wellman is co-director of MiraVia LLC. He consults and presents for school systems, professional groups and publishers throughout the United States and Canada, presenting workshops and courses for teachers and administrators on interactive and collaborative instruction, thinking skills development, learning-focused conversations for supervisors and mentors, presentation skills and facilitating collaborative groups. Mr. Wellman has served as a classroom teacher, curriculum coordinator, and staff developer in the Oberlin, Ohio and Concord, Massachusetts public schools. He holds a B.A. degree from Antioch College and a M.Ed. from Lesley College. He lives with his wife Leslie Cowperthwaite in southern Vermont, where they enjoy gardening and natural history.

The Adaptive School: Developing and Facilitating Collaborative Groups . Center for Adaptive Schools . www.adaptive-schools.com

ii

Preface

This edition represents much of our learning about school systems and groups in the past 15 years of working with educators in settings that span the globe. Although each school is unique, there are social patterns that are easily recognizable when people gather in groups to work together. Drawing on these experiences and looking at group work through the theoretical filters of biology, ecology, quantum physics, complexity science, systems thinking, and cognitive and social pyschology we offer a practical set of principles and tools for developing and facilitating collaborative groups.

The Adaptive School is about developing strong schools in which collaborative faculties are capable of meeting the certain challenges of today and the uncertain challenges of tomorrow. Some schools are flourishing. Others are making remarkable gains in improving student achievement, increasing attendance, attaining higher post-school accomplishments, and developing satisfying relationships with communities. Some schools produce only fair results; others languish. We believe that all can be better.

As realists, we recognize that difficult and different challenges beset schools and communities in their quest to serve students. Issues differ. Urbanism and ruralism bring their own special problems. Defeatism, extremism, apathy, or politics infect some schools. Some schools become obsessed with ensuring preditable results. Others struggle to overcome the effects of extreme poverty, neglected children, or the burdens of ponderous bureaucracy. Money can bring its own problems. Some affluent communities lobby for traditional definitions of success at the expense of other needs. In some districts teachers and students struggle daily with inadequate and outdated materials and facilities. Regardless of the nature of the issues, our premise is that the means for improvement exist within the school community. The practical ideas and tools in this book show how to activate these resources if they are dormant and focus them if they are scattered.

We believe that leadership is important and that the most effective leadership is informed, deeply developed, and widely distributed. To be adaptive and meet the demands of omnipresent change requires more than linear thought, tired problem-solving formulas, and recycled strategic plans. In the work of school improvement, human energy matters as much as the elements of good management. Maybe more.

The Adaptive School: Developing and Facilitating Collaborative Groups . Center for Adaptive Schools . www.adaptive-schools.com

iii

Table of Contents

The Adaptive School: Developing and Facilitating Collaborative Groups . Center for Adaptive Schools . www.adaptive-schools.com

iv

The Adaptive School: Developing and Facilitating Collaborative Groups . Center for Adaptive Schools . www.adaptive-schools.com

v

The Adaptive School: Developing and Facilitating Collaborative Groups . Center for Adaptive Schools . www.adaptive-schools.com

vi

The Adaptive School: Developing and Facilitating Collaborative Groups . Center for Adaptive Schools . www.adaptive-schools.com

viii

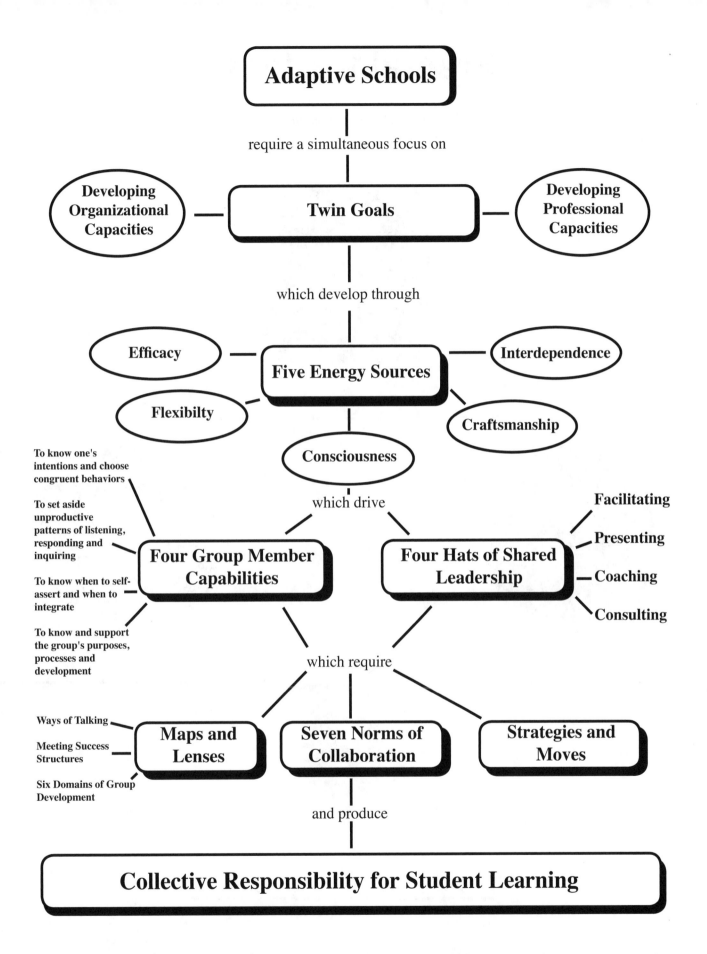

Adaptive Schools

require a simultaneous focus on

Developing Organizational Capacities — **Twin Goals** — Developing Professional Capacities

which develop through

Efficacy — **Five Energy Sources** — Interdependence

Flexibilty

Craftsmanship

Consciousness

which drive

To know one's intentions and choose congruent behaviors

To set aside unproductive patterns of listening, responding and inquiring

To know when to self-assert and when to integrate

To know and support the group's purposes, processes and development

Four Group Member Capabilities

Four Hats of Shared Leadership

Facilitating

Presenting

Coaching

Consulting

which require

Ways of Talking

Meeting Success Structures

Six Domains of Group Development

Maps and Lenses

Seven Norms of Collaboration

Strategies and Moves

and produce

Collective Responsibility for Student Learning

The Adaptive School: Developing and Facilitating Collaborative Groups . Center for Adaptive Schools . www.adaptive-schools.com

Fractal Partners

Make an appointment with four different people, one for each slot. Be sure you each record the appointment on your page in the corresponding slot.

#2 _Janie_

#2 Mary
(Trudy)
on Fri.

Michelle Perez

#10 _Angelica_

The Adaptive School: Developing and Facilitating Collaborative Groups . Center for Adaptive Schools . www.adaptive-schools.com

2

Clock Partners

Make an appointment with four different people, one for each indicated hour on the clock. Be sure you each record the appointment on your clocks in the corresponding slot.

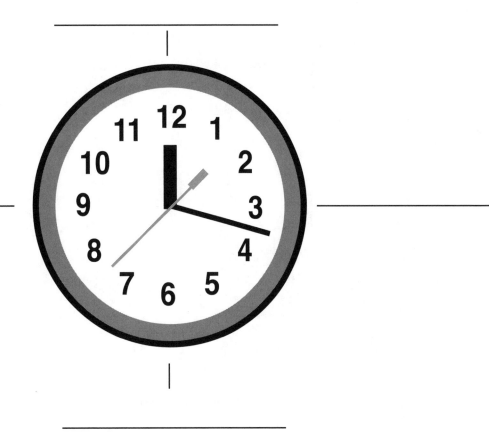

The Adaptive School: Developing and Facilitating Collaborative Groups . Center for Adaptive Schools . www.adaptive-schools.com

3

Strategies

See The Adaptive School: A Sourcebook for Developing Collaborative Groups Appendix A for strategy descriptions

The Adaptive School: Developing and Facilitating Collaborative Groups . Center for Adaptive Schools . www.adaptive-schools.com

4

Strategies

The Adaptive School: Developing and Facilitating Collaborative Groups . Center for Adaptive Schools . www.adaptive-schools.com

6

Strategies

The Adaptive School: Developing and Facilitating Collaborative Groups . Center for Adaptive Schools . www.adaptive-schools.com

7

The Adaptive School

The central survival skill is surely the capacity to pay attention and respond to changing circumstances, to learn and adapt, to fit into new environments beyond the safety of the temple precincts.   Mary Catherine Bateson

The Adaptive School: Developing and Facilitating Collaborative Groups . Center for Adaptive Schools . www.adaptive-schools.com

9

Three Focus Areas

Productive group work is organized by three focus areas:
- Facilitating groups
- Developing groups
- Becoming a more skillful group member

These three arenas are essential focus areas for all successful groups. This seminar offers concepts, tips and tools for extending and refining skills in each of these territories.

Facilitating Groups

Facilitation is an act of planned improvisation. Skilled and confident facilitators pay attention to several dimensions simultaneously: task focus, process-skills development and relationships within the group. With appropriate maps and tools, knowledgeable facilitators are able to anticipate what might happen during a session; monitor in-the-moment activities and actions and monitor where such actions fit within the bigger picture for the group and for the organization; and recover when the group, group members, or they themselves lose focus and direction.

Developing Groups

Our basic premise is that groups develop from novice to more expert levels of performance. Expertise does not always result from time together or from basic levels of task completion. Expert groups consciously develop their capacities and toolkits for engaging in more complex work and more emotionally challenging tasks. One hallmark of emerging expertise is a group's willingness to take time to reflect on it's processes, products and development as a group. Group development is the shared responsibility of the group leaders, group facilitators and group members.

Becoming a More Skillful Group Member

At a fundamental level there is no such thing as group behavior, there are only the choices that individuals make about what to say or do and what they choose not to say or do. Expert group members employ a well-crafted set of verbal and nonverbal tools to productively influence the thinking, decisions and choices of others in the group. They also monitor the effects of their choices on themselves and the impacts of their actions as other group members respond or choose not to respond to these actions. Skillful group members help the group and the facilitator maintain focus, momentum and outcome achievement.

The Adaptive School: Developing and Facilitating Collaborative Groups . Center for Adaptive Schools . www.adaptive-schools.com

10

Adaptive Schools and Professional Community

Adaptive Schools

- **Adaptive:** *changing form, clarifying identity*

- **Dynamical principles**
  - *More data do not lead to better predictions.*
  - *Everything influences everything else.*
  - *Tiny events produce major disturbances.*
  - *You don't have to touch everyone to make a difference.*
  - *Both things and energy matter.*

- **Focusing questions**
  - *Who are we?*
  - *Why are we doing this?*
  - *Why are we doing this this way?*

Increased Student Learning

Professional Community

- **Compelling purpose, shared standards, and academic focus**

- **Collective efficacy and shared responsibility for student learning**

- **Collaborative culture**

- **Communal application of effective teaching practices and deprivatized practice**

- **Relational trust in one another, in students, and in parents**

- **Individual and group learning based on ongoing assessment and feedback**

The Adaptive School: Developing and Facilitating Collaborative Groups . Center for Adaptive Schools . www.adaptive-schools.com

11

The Elements of Professional Community

The emerging research base supports the importance of the essential elements of professional community. We are drawing here from three arenas: (a) research on the effects of the adult culture on student learning, (b) research on the impacts of teacher collective efficacy on student learning, and (c) research on the effects of teachers' academic optimism on student learning.

1. Compelling purpose, shared standards, and academic focus

Communities come into existence and thrive because of a common purpose for working together. A group's compelling purpose establishes reciprocal expectations for its members. Louis, Marks, and Kruse (1996) assert that teachers' professional communities operate with a sense of moral authority and moral responsibility for making a difference in the lives of students. Such purpose must be grounded in clearly articulated standards for both student and teacher performance. Defining and refining the meaning of doing good work is the task of a professional learning community. Understandable performance and product standards are an important catalyst for conversations among colleagues and for focusing conversations with students and parents.

The work on academic optimism by Hoy, Tarter, and Woolfolk-Hoy (2006) emphasizes the significance of establishing and maintaining a strong academic focus in the school and is at the center of the work of any professional community. Without such a focus, groups spend their time talking about and around peripheral issues instead of working on the work of learning and teaching.

2. Collective efficacy and shared responsibility for student learning

The personal efficacy of individual teachers is a well-studied phenomenon (Tschannen-Moran, Woolfolk-Hoy, & Hoy, 1998). Highly efficacious teachers believe that their teaching knowledge and skills can overcome external factors to make an important difference for their students. Teachers with stronger personal efficacy beliefs consistently outperform teachers in the same settings with weaker beliefs.

These applications in education are based on the concepts of self-efficacy that Albert Bandura (1977) introduced more than a quarter century ago. Self-efficacy is the belief in our capacity to organize and carry out a plan of action to produce some goal.

More recent work (Goddard, Hoy, & Woolfolk-Hoy, 2004) extends these concepts into the collective realm of teaching. To have a high degree of collective efficacy means that group members believe that they and others, individually and together, are capable of producing increased student success and of overcoming obstacles to that goal. These collective expectations are a powerful element in a school and in a team's working culture, influencing the behaviors and choices of both the individuals and the group as a whole.

Goddard, Hoy and Woolfolk-Hoy (2004) report that being able to influence instructionally relevant school decisions is the most important factor in developing a robust sense of collective efficacy. Participating in decision making contributes strongly to teachers' beliefs in the capabilities of their peers, fosters commitment to school goals, and promotes gains in student achievement.

The Adaptive School: Developing and Facilitating Collaborative Groups . Center for Adaptive Schools . www.adaptive-schools.com

12

3. Collaborative culture

Who teachers are to one another is as important as who they are to their students. In high-performing and improving schools, studies show that collaboration is the norm (Little, 1982; Newman & Associates, 1997). We are not talking here about project-based collaboration or the "contrived collegiality" described by Hargreaves and Dawe (1990) in which administrators create tasks and agendas to occupy teachers' collective energies. Rather, we are referring to sharing expertise and perspectives on teaching and learning processes, examining data on students, and developing a sense of mutual support and shared responsibility for effective instruction.

Collaboration and collegiality in this way are part of one's professional identity. Collaboration does not happen by chance; it has to be taught, practiced, and learned. Developing collaborative cultures is the work of leaders who realize that a collection of superstar teachers working in isolation cannot produce the same results as interdependent colleagues who share and develop professional practices together. From such interactions come growth and learning for teachers, teams, and schools as adaptive organizations.

4. Communal application of effective teaching practices and deprivatized practice

The norm of privacy has deep roots in "real" schools." Once the classroom door is closed, the teacher is God. In this sphere of autonomy lies both greatness and sorrow. Within the zone of isolation, some teachers still find ways to develop craft knowledge, content knowledge, and compassion for their students. These extraordinary individuals manage to stimulate their teaching and continually renew their passion for daily interactions with young minds. All too often, however, this same isolation buffers mediocrity and hides high performers from those who might learn from their modeling, consultation, and coaching.

When practice is deprivatized, teachers visit one another's classrooms to observe master teaching, to coach one another, to mentor, and to solve problems in the living laboratory of instructional space. Students are the beneficiaries of shared teaching repertoires. Although many schools and districts have spent much time and energy developing coherent curriculum maps, shared instructional maps are equally important. When students proceed to the next grade or next subject in a secondary school, having possession of a predictable learning repertoire (such as an understanding of a palette of graphic organizers) energizes learning and increases success—especially for the least successful learners. By developing communities of practice, teachers establish a working zone between the macroworld of district initiatives and resources and the microworld of their classrooms (McLaughlin & Talbert, 2006). In this way they develop more coherent instructional approaches that represent a shared understanding of their unique setting.

The Adaptive School: Developing and Facilitating Collaborative Groups . Center for Adaptive Schools . www.adaptive-schools.com

13

5. Relational trust in one another, in students and parents.

In their work on the effects of academic optimism on student achievement Hoy, Tarter, & Woolfolk-Hoy (2006) point out that collective efficacy is the cognitive side of the equation, academic emphasis is the behavioral side, and faculty trust in one another, in students, and in parents is the affective side. Given the powerful biochemical connections between thinking and feeling in our bodies and our brains, it is difficult to separate these functions in practice. Trust is the glue that binds community members to one another. This is equally true for teacher communities, classroom communities, and parent communities. When all three parties hold the expectations for their relationships, and these expectations are grounded in shared goals and values, trust is a powerful resource for learning.

Bryk and Schneider (2002), in their seminal work in Chicago schools, name four elements of relational trust: respect, competence, personal regard for others, and integrity. Respect comes in the form of basic civility and a willingness to listen deeply to what each person has to say. Parents, students, and teachers need opportunities to talk with and influence each other and to believe that they can positively affect educational outcomes. Competence is the sense that each party has the ability to carry out its appropriate roles and produce desired outcomes. This applies to both academic results and teacher-student relationships. When gross incompetence goes unchecked, it erodes trust and undermines shared efforts toward improving learning. Personal regard for others deepens relational trust. We are a social species, wired for relationships and reciprocity. Mutual support and mutual caring fuel these associations. Extending ourselves to and for others is like making a deposit in the trust account; the interest in this account compounds with each deposit. Integrity is the congruence between saying and doing. In trusting relationships, this means we believe that a sense of morality and ethics is operating in others and in the ways we are relating. Following through with agreements and commitments is a key aspect of integrity.

6. Individual and group learning based on ongoing assessment and feedback

"Learning is a basic, adaptive function of humans. More than any other species, people are designed to be flexible learners and active agents in acquiring knowledge and skills" (Bransford, Brown, & Cocking, 1999, p, xi). Cognitive science tells us that learning is socially constructed and individually integrated; learning therefore requires engaging with other learners and is an active process for all involved. Individual and collective learning is one of the key characteristics of effective professional learning communities (Bolam, McMahon, Stoll, Thomas, & Wallace, 2005).

For adult groups, learning how to learn together requires conscious attention, purposeful structures, and meaningful feedback. One form of feedback arises when teachers look at student work together to explore what is working and what might require modification in their curricular and instructional approaches. Groups apply another form of feedback when they take time to reflect on their own processes and outcomes to consider which practices to continue, which to abandon, and which to modify.

From time to time a group or team will share with us that it has some great number of years of combined teaching experience. Their assumption is that learning is additive, when in fact the group members have merely been involved in side-by-side processes. Engaging in parallel play without feedback and reflection is usually a poor teacher.

The Adaptive School: Developing and Facilitating Collaborative Groups . Center for Adaptive Schools . www.adaptive-schools.com

14

Group Member Capabilities

1. To know ones' intentions and choose congruent behaviors

2. To set aside unproductive patterns of listening, responding and inquiring

    - *Autobiographical*
    - *Inquisitive*
    - *Solution*

3. To know when to self-assert and when to integrate

4. To know and support the group's purposes, topics, processes and development

The Adaptive School: Developing and Facilitating Collaborative Groups . Center for Adaptive Schools . www.adaptive-schools.com

15

Adaptive Schools

Developing Organizational Capacities

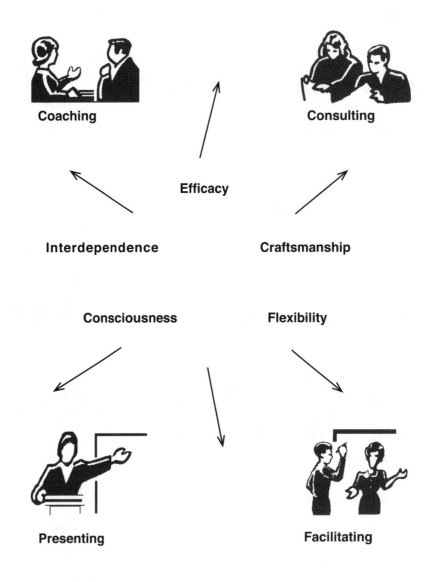

Coaching

Consulting

Efficacy

Interdependence

Craftsmanship

Consciousness

Flexibility

Presenting

Facilitating

Developing Professional Capacities

The Adaptive School: Developing and Facilitating Collaborative Groups . Center for Adaptive Schools . www.adaptive-schools.com

16

Four Hats of Shared Leadership

In an adaptive organization, leadership is shared—all the players wear all the hats. All participants must have the knowledge and skills to manage themselves and to manage and lead others. Leadership is a shared function in meetings, in staff development activities, in action research and in projects. Recognizing the hats and knowing when and how to change them is shared knowledge within the organization, because when values, roles and work relationships are clear, decisions about appropriate behavior are easy. We offer definitions to illustrate the major functions of the four leadership roles and the distinctions between these roles.

Facilitating

To *facilitate* means "make easier". A facilitator conducts a meeting in which the purpose may be dialogue, shared decision making, planning or problem solving. The facilitator directs the procedures to be used in the meeting, choreographs the energy within the group, and maintains a focus on one content and one process at a time. The facilitator should rarely be the person in the group with the greatest role or knowledge authority.

Presenting

To *present* is to teach. A presenter's goals are to extend and enrich knowledge, skills, or attitudes and to help these to be applied in people's work. A presenter may adopt many stances (expert, colleague, novice, or friend) and use many strategies of presentation (lecture, cooperative learning, or study groups). Premier presenters are guided by clarity of instructional outcomes and the continual assessment of goal achievement.

Coaching

To *coach* is to help a group take action toward its goals while simultaneously helping it to develop expertise in planning, reflecting, problem solving and decision making. The coach takes a nonjudgmental stance and uses the tools of, pausing, paraphrasing, inquiry and probing for specificity. The skillful coach focuses on the perceptions of group members and their thinking and decision-making processes to develop the resources for self-directed learning.

Consulting

A *consultant* can be an information specialist or an advocate for content or process. As an information specialist, the consultant delivers technical knowledge to a group. As a content advocate, the consultant encourages group members to use a certain strategy, adopt a particular program, or purchase a specific brand of equipment or materials. As a process advocate, the consultant attempts to influence the group's methodology (for example, recommending an open meeting rather than a closed one in order to increase trust in the system). To effectively consult, one must have trust, commonly defined goals and the group's desired outcomes clearly in mind.

The Adaptive School: Developing and Facilitating Collaborative Groups . Center for Adaptive Schools . www.adaptive-schools.com

17

Applying Microskills Across Four Hats

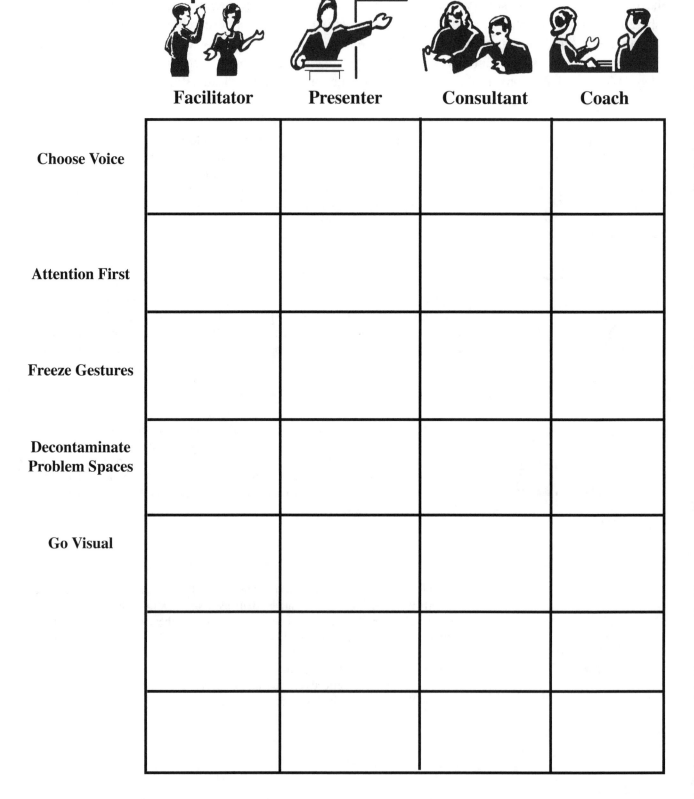

	Facilitator	Presenter	Consultant	Coach
Choose Voice				
Attention First				
Freeze Gestures				
Decontaminate Problem Spaces				
Go Visual				

The Adaptive School: Developing and Facilitating Collaborative Groups . Center for Adaptive Schools . www.adaptive-schools.com

18

Holonomy and the Five Energy Sources

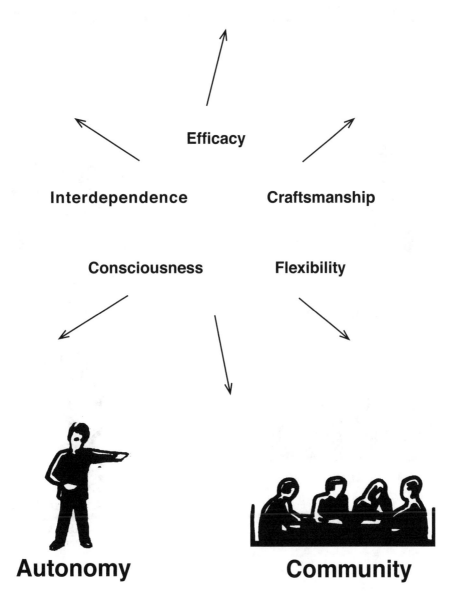

Efficacy

Interdependence

Craftsmanship

Consciousness

Flexibility

Autonomy

Community

Holonomy: From the Greek, *holos*, meaning a "whole" and *on* meaning "part", holonomy refers to the realization that elements are at the same time parts of a bigger system and yet entire systems within themselves. Effective systems seek resolutions to the conflicting tensions between part and whole, independence and interdependence.

The Adaptive School: Developing and Facilitating Collaborative Groups . Center for Adaptive Schools . www.adaptive-schools.com

19

Six Organizational Capacities

Vision, Values and Goal Focus

Initiating and managing adaptation

Interpreting and using data

Developing and maintaining collaborative cultures

Gathering and focusing resources

Systems Thinking

The Adaptive School: Developing and Facilitating Collaborative Groups . Center for Adaptive Schools . www.adaptive-schools.com

20

Six Professional Capacities

Collegial Interaction

Knowledge of the structure of the discipline(s)

**Self-knowledge
Values
Standards
Beliefs**

Repertoire of teaching skills

Knowing about students and how they learn

Cognitive Processes of Instruction

The Adaptive School: Developing and Facilitating Collaborative Groups . Center for Adaptive Schools . www.adaptive-schools.com

21

Five Energy Sources for High-Performing Groups

- **Efficacy**
- **Flexibility**
- **Craftsmanship**
- **Consciousness**
- **Interdependence**

All groups confront two major sets of problems:

1. Adapting and surviving in the external environment

2. Developing internally to support daily functioning and the capacity to adapt

Groups evolve either toward inclusion and effectiveness or devolve into fragmentation and disarray

Changing the structure of groups or teaching group members skills does not guarantee growth and increasing effectiveness. Skilled group developers focus group member attention on these basic energy sources to expand the group's capacity to grow and learn from its experiences.

The following pages illustrate points of diagnosis and potential intervention for group development. Group development accelerates through four intervention approaches:

1. Teaching about the energy sources

2. Structuring the environment to support selected energy sources

3. Mediating selected energy sources at strategic intervention points

4. Monitoring evidence and artifacts of selected energy sources

> *What we see is most influenced by who we have decided to be.*
> Margaret Wheatley and Myron Kellner-Rogers

The following work on the five energy sources is adapted from Costa and Garmston (2002)

The Adaptive School: Developing and Facilitating Collaborative Groups . Center for Adaptive Schools . www.adaptive-schools.com

22

Five Energy Sources for High-Performing Groups

Efficacy

The group believes in its capacity to produce results and stays the course through internal and external difficulties to achieve its goals. The group aligns energies within itself and outside itself in pursuit of its outcomes.

Flexibility

The group regards situations from multiple perspectives, works creatively with uncertainty and ambiguity and values and utilizes differences within itself and the larger community of which it is a part. The group attends to rational and intuitive ways of working.

Craftsmanship

The group strives for clarity in its values, goals and high standards. It applies these as criteria for its planning, actions, reflections and refinements. It attends to both short- and long-term time perspectives. It continuously refines communications processes within and beyond the group.

Consciousness

The group monitors its decisions, actions and reflections based on its values, norms and common goals. Members are aware of the impact their actions have on one another, the total group and individuals and groups beyond this immediate group.

Interdependence

The group values its internal and external relationships. It seeks reciprocal influence and learning. The members treat conflict as opportunities to improve and learn about themselves, their own group and other groups. The group trusts its interactions and the processes of dialogue.

The Adaptive School: Developing and Facilitating Collaborative Groups . Center for Adaptive Schools . www.adaptive-schools.com

23

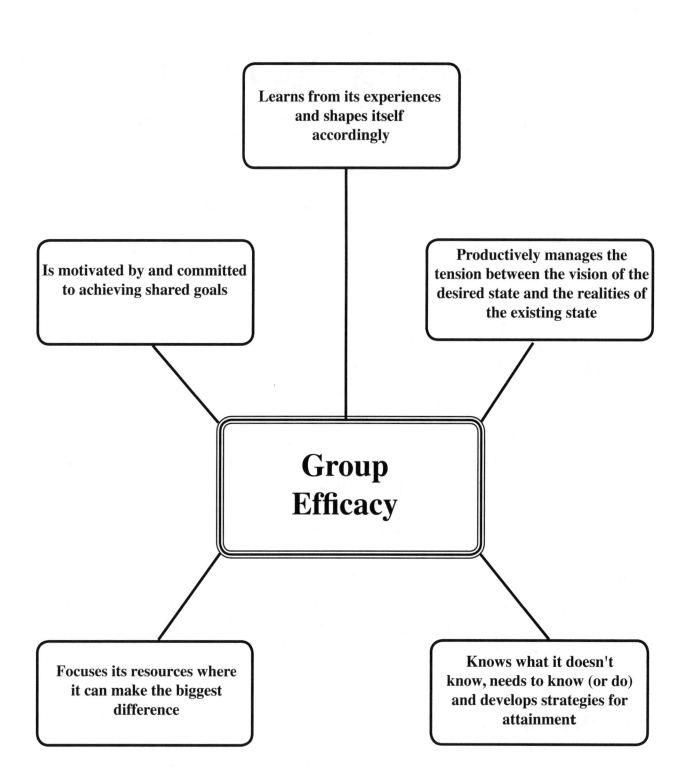

Learns from its experiences and shapes itself accordingly

Is motivated by and committed to achieving shared goals

Productively manages the tension between the vision of the desired state and the realities of the existing state

Group Efficacy

Focuses its resources where it can make the biggest difference

Knows what it doesn't know, needs to know (or do) and develops strategies for attainment

The Adaptive School: Developing and Facilitating Collaborative Groups . Center for Adaptive Schools . www.adaptive-schools.com

24

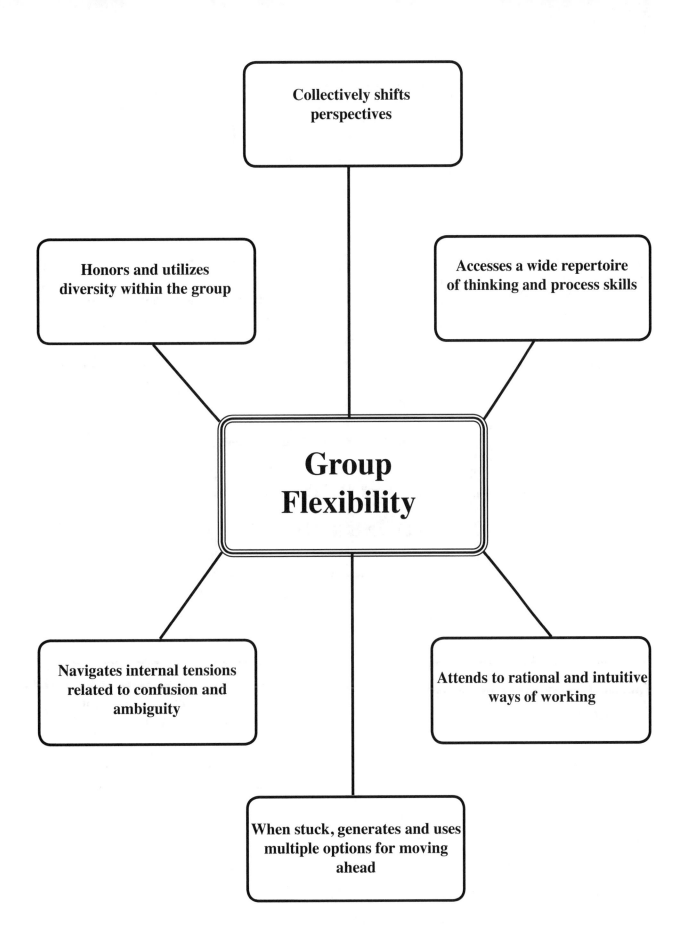

The Adaptive School: Developing and Facilitating Collaborative Groups . Center for Adaptive Schools . www.adaptive-schools.com

25

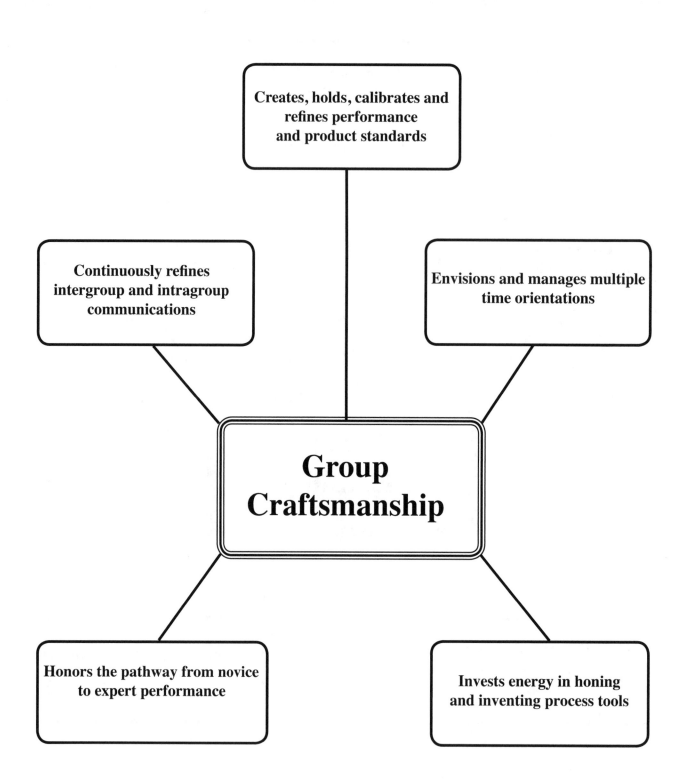

Creates, holds, calibrates and refines performance and product standards

Continuously refines intergroup and intragroup communications

Envisions and manages multiple time orientations

Group Craftsmanship

Honors the pathway from novice to expert performance

Invests energy in honing and inventing process tools

The Adaptive School: Developing and Facilitating Collaborative Groups . Center for Adaptive Schools . www.adaptive-schools.com

26

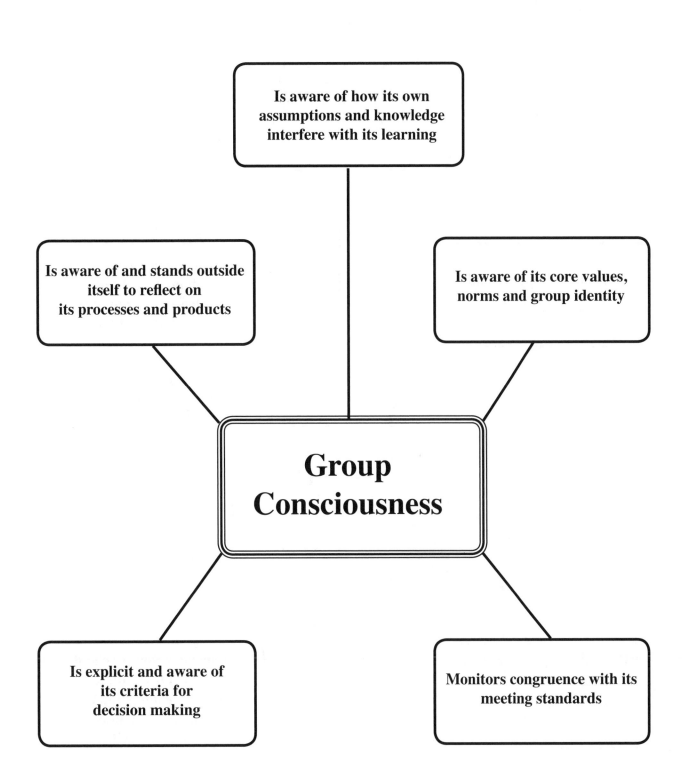

Is aware of how its own assumptions and knowledge interfere with its learning

Is aware of and stands outside itself to reflect on its processes and products

Is aware of its core values, norms and group identity

Group Consciousness

Is explicit and aware of its criteria for decision making

Monitors congruence with its meeting standards

The Adaptive School: Developing and Facilitating Collaborative Groups . Center for Adaptive Schools . www.adaptive-schools.com

27

```
                    ┌─────────────────────────────┐
                    │  Values its interactions and trusts │
                    │  the processes of dialogue    │
                    └─────────────────────────────┘
                                   │
┌──────────────────────┐          │          ┌──────────────────────────┐
│  Envisions the potential │       │          │ Is aware of its relationships and │
│  of the group         │          │          │ how its webs of           │
└──────────────────────┘          │          │ interconnections are       │
                      \            │          │ sources of mutual influence │
                       \           │         /└──────────────────────────┘
                        \    ┌─────────────────────┐  /
                         \   ║                     ║ /
                          \  ║       Group         ║/
                             ║   Interdependence   ║
                          /  ║                     ║\
                         /   └─────────────────────┘ \
                        /              │               \
┌──────────────────────┐              │          ┌──────────────────────────┐
│  Regards disagreement and │          │          │  Regards knowledge and    │
│  conflict as a source of learning │  │          │  knowing as fluid,         │
│  and transformation for the │       │          │  provisional and subject to │
│  group                │                          │  improvement from information │
└──────────────────────┘                          │  outside itself            │
                                                   └──────────────────────────┘
```

The Adaptive School: Developing and Facilitating Collaborative Groups . Center for Adaptive Schools . www.adaptive-schools.com

28

The Adaptive School: Developing and Facilitating Collaborative Groups . Center for Adaptive Schools . www.adaptive-schools.com

30

Ways of Talking

Tell me what you pay attention to and I will tell you who your are.
Jose Ortega y Gasset

The Adaptive School: Developing and Facilitating Collaborative Groups . Center for Adaptive Schools . www.adaptive-schools.com

31

Ways of Talking

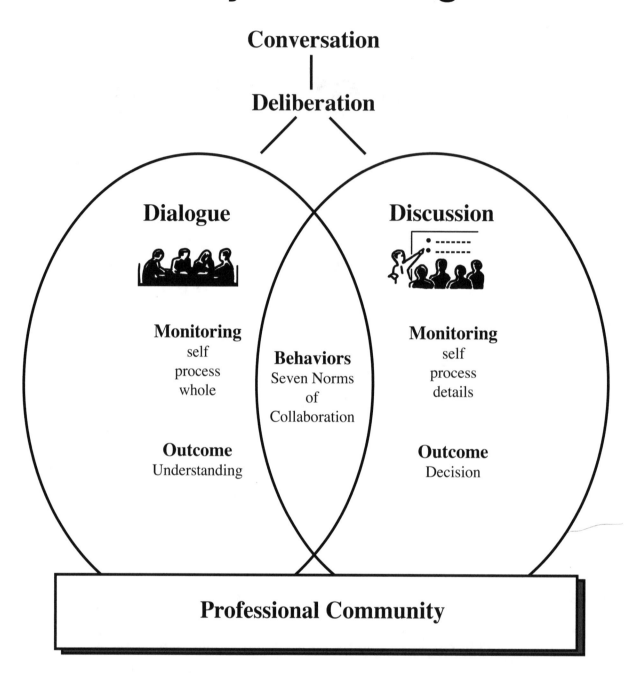

Conversation

Deliberation

Dialogue

Discussion

Monitoring
self
process
whole

Behaviors
Seven Norms
of
Collaboration

Monitoring
self
process
details

Outcome
Understanding

Outcome
Decision

Professional Community

The Adaptive School: Developing and Facilitating Collaborative Groups . Center for Adaptive Schools . www.adaptive-schools.com

32

Ways of Talking

In order to have a conversation with someone you must reveal yourself.

--- James Baldwin

Professional communities are born and nurtured in webs of conversation. What we talk about in our schools and how we talk about those things says much about who we are, who we think we are and who we wish to be, both in the moment and in the collective future that we are creating for ourselves as colleagues and for the students we serve.

To develop shared understanding and be ready to take collective action, working groups need knowledge and skill in two ways of talking. One way of talking, dialogue, leads to collective meaning making and the development of shared understanding. The other way of talking, discussion, leads to decisions that stay made.

Dialogue honors the social-emotional brain, building a sense of connection, belonging and safety. As a shape for conversations, it connects us to our underlying motivations and mental models. This way of talking forms a foundation for coherent sustained effort and community building. In dialogue we hear phases like "An assumption I have is…." and, "I'd be curious to hear what other people are thinking about this issue."

Discussion in its more skillful form requires conversations that are infused with sustained critical thinking, careful consideration of options and respect for conflicting points of view. This way of talking leads to decision making that serves the group's and the school's vision, values and goals. In a discussion we hear phrases like "We need to define the problem we are solving before jumping to solutions" and "I'd like to see the data that these assumptions are based on before we go much further."

Conversation and Deliberation

When groups come together they "converge" and "converse". These words' respective Latin roots means that group members "turn together" and "associate with one another." Conversation is informal talking in which participants share information, anecdotes and opinions to learn from one another or simply to enjoy one another's company. When the conversation takes on an organized purpose to either deepen understanding or make a decision, a group that understands that there are two ways of talking acknowledges this point of deliberation and consciously chooses to engage in either dialogue or discussion. Deliberation, in its Latin root, *deliberare*, means to weigh, as in to evaluate, assess, or ponder.

The Adaptive School: Developing and Facilitating Collaborative Groups . Center for Adaptive Schools . www.adaptive-schools.com

33

Group members have this choice point available to them only when they have road maps for ways of talking and consciousness about group processes and group purposes. A significant part of this awareness is recognizing that culturally embedded patterns shape behaviors – patterns from the larger surrounding culture and patterns from organizational and group culture. Many groups default into the Western cultural habit of polarized discussion and debate. Our media-saturated world bombards us with arguments framed by commentators as point-counterpoint, pro and con, left versus right, and other polarities. These models transfer to conversations in working groups; they then frame how participants listen to others and how and when participants speak. If group members are not careful, they end up listening not to understand but to hear gaps in the logic of other speakers, or they interrupt to make a point even before the current speaker is finished. Conversations then break down into verbal combat with winners and losers.

All too often, valued colleagues become conscientious objectors, choosing not to participate in the fray. The group then loses perspective and potential alternative viewpoints. The loudest and most persistent voices become the policy makers, and in the worst cases, the process sows the seeds of passive noncompliance or sabotage in those who feel excluded or devalued.

When groups understand that they have more than one way of talking available to them, they can then choose to pursue the path of dialogue or to follow the path of discussion. Most important issues require explorations along both pathways. Many sensitive issues, especially those with high stakes for the participants, call for separate sessions in which the dialogue and discussion are separated in time and sometimes space. One useful facilitation technique is to explicitly label agenda items as either dialogue or discussion and offer language models to further mark the distinctions between the two forms of discourse.

As group members become more sophisticated with the ways of talking, the pathways become more malleable. For example, during a dialogue, a group member senses an emerging consensus on an issue. He or she then inquires if this is so and frames a proposal to move the item to a decision. In another case, during a discussion, emotions rise and the details become muddled. Someone then proposes that the group switch to a dialogue format for a set time to explore the feelings and underlying issues that are present.

The Path of Dialogue

Dialogue is a reflective learning process in which group members seek to understand one another's viewpoints and deeply held assumptions. The word dialogue comes from the Greek *dialogos*. *Dia* means "through" and *logos* means "word." In this meaning-making through words, group members inquire into their own and others' beliefs, values, and mental models to better understand how things work in their world. In dialogue, listening is as important as speaking. For skilled group members, much of the work is done internally.

Physicist and philosopher David Bohm(1990) described dialogue as a process of surfacing and altering the "tacit infrastructure of thought." As a quantum physicist, Bohm draws an analogy between dialogue and superconductivity. Electrons that are cooled to extremely low temperatures dramatically change their behavior, operating more as a coherent whole and less as separate parts.

The Adaptive School: Developing and Facilitating Collaborative Groups . Center for Adaptive Schools . www.adaptive-schools.com

34

environments, electrons flow around barriers and one another without resistance, creating very high energy. The same electrons radically change behavior in a new environment. At higher temperatures they operate as separate entities with random movement and loss of momentum.

Dialogue creates an emotional and cognitive safety zone in which ideas flow for examination without judgment. Although many of the capabilities and tools of dialogue and skilled discussion are the same, their core intentions are quite different and require different personal and collective monitoring processes.

Monitoring Dialogue
Mindful group members pay attention to three essential elements during productive dialogue. They monitor themselves, the process of the dialogue and the new whole that is emerging within the group.

Self
Dialogue is first and foremost a listening practice. When we "listen to our listening" we notice whether we are internally debating with the speaker, reviewing our mental catalogue of related information and personal anecdotes, or composing a response. Noticing these common internal processes allows us to switch them off so that we can hear others without judging.

Dialogue requires choice making. Typical choices include how and when to talk ---- Do we paraphrase prior comments to check for understanding and or synthesize? Do we inquire into the ideas and assumptions of others? Or, do we put a new idea or perspective on the table to widen the frame?

Suspension is an essential internal skill in dialogue. To suspend judgment, group members temporarily set aside their own perceptions, feelings, and impulses and carefully monitor their internal experience. Points of personal conflict can easily emerge when we believe that others are not hearing us or that they are distorting our point of view. Points of conflict also surface when our own values conflict with those of a speaker. These areas of discomfort influence our listening and our responses, which in turn influence the thoughts and behaviors of other group members.

Peter Senge (1994) notes that suspension also involves developing an awareness of our own assumptions and purposely "hanging them from the ceiling" – , that is suspending them in front of the group so that all can examine them. These assumptions are beliefs --- often unexamined--- about why we think things work as they do. Our assumptions drive our perceptions, simultaneously opening and blinding us to possibilities in the world around us.

Process
Dialogue as a process requires focusing on the goal of developing shared understanding. In our action-oriented work environments, this is often countercultural. Yet, in every group with which we've worked, all the participants could recite examples of decisions that were poorly conceived, poorly communicated, simply ignored or in the worst cases violated by many organizational members without consequence. At the root of all these stories were group processes that were not thought out but rather often hurried and inappropriately facilitated. The rush to action pushed unclear decision-making processes and timelines onto the group without sufficient attention to developing ashared understanding of both problems and solutions.

The Adaptive School: Developing and Facilitating Collaborative Groups . Center for Adaptive Schools . www.adaptive-schools.com

35

By going slow and honoring the flow of dialogue, groups can often go fast when they get to the choice points in decision-making. When the assumptions and the implications of those assumptions have been explored during dialogue, group members don't second-guess the motives of others during discussions.

Meetings should be safe but not necessarily comfortable. When a group confuses safety with comfort, it sacrifices productive tension for the ease of conviviality. Humor and banter can be avoidance strategies as much as they can be social lubricants. A lack of comfort with discomfort weakens dialogue and undermines the learning possibilities in that moment.

Whole

Thought is both a personal and a collective process. We influence and are influenced in turn by others. During dialogue, the line between self and others blurs when we open ourselves to the possibilities within the communal thought space. This created whole is in itself a goal of dialogue. Communities move forward together. Collective understanding leads to shared goals and shared practices that tap the power of cumulative effect for student learning and for the adult learning community.

The whole is always greater than the sum of the individual parts. In many ways it is both process and product simultaneously. By learning to observe the processes, patterns and results that emerge from our dialogues, we can more consciously participate and more consciously contribute to the whole of which we are the parts.

Understanding as the Outcome

Well-crafted dialogue leads to understanding. This is the foundation for conflict resolution, consensus and professional community. Decisions that don't stay made are often the result of group members feeling left out and or having their ideas discounted by the group. Dialogue gives voice to all parties and all viewpoints.

Misunderstanding lies beneath most intragroup and intergroup conflict. Dialogue illuminates and clarifies misunderstandings when the underlying values and beliefs are brought to the surface for examination. There is often alignment at this level; it is at the solution level that opinions differ. Working from a foundation of shared understanding, group members can more easily and rationally resolve differences, generate options, and make wise choices when they move to the discussion side of the journey.

The Path of Discussion

Discussion, in its Latin root *discutere,* means "to shake apart." It focuses on the parts and their relationships to one another – the causes, the effects and the ripple effects of proposed actions and solutions. In its most ineffective forms, discussion consists of serial sharing and serial advocacy without much group-member inquiry into the thinking and proposals of others. Participants attempt to reach decisions through a variety of voting and consensus techniques. When discussion is unskilled and dialogue is absent, decisions are often low-quality, represent the opinions of the most vocal members or leader, lack group commitment, and do not stay made.

With unskilled discussion or lil dialoge, decisions are often bad, not representative of group, w/o commitmen & don't stay made

The Adaptive School: Developing and Facilitating Collaborative Groups . Center for Adaptive Schools . www.adaptive-schools.com

36

Three elements *shape* skilled discussions: (a) clarity about decision-making processes and authority, (b) knowledge of the boundaries surrounding the topics open to the group's decision-making authority, and (c) standards for orderly decision-making meetings. Most meetings are, in fact, structured discussions.

Monitoring Discussion

Mindful group members pay attention to three essential elements during productive discussion. They monitor themselves, the processes of skilled discussion and the details of the problem-solving, planning and decision-making processes in which they are engaged.

Self

Productive discussions require group members to have emotional and mental flexibility. When our goal is to influence the thinking of others and we give up the model of "winning and losing", we are more able to notice our thoughts and actions and the effects of those thoughts and actions on others.

Mentally, this requires taking a balcony view. This perceptual position is neither *egocentric* (I am intensely aware of my thoughts, feelings, and intentions and know my own boundaries) nor *allocentric* (I am aware of how something looks, feels, and sounds from the point of view of another). The balcony view is a third perceptual position, a *macrocentric* perspective, in which with compassion and detachment we try to understand the nature of the situation the group is in at the moment. It is with this view, looking down upon the group, that we gain the most knowledge about our group, the group's interactions, and ourselves.

From the balcony we can make the most strategic choices about how and when to participate. Should I advocate or should I inquire? At what points should I press? When should I probe for detail or let go? How might I phrase an idea for greatest influence? These are the same internal skills that teachers employ when they monitor and adjust in their classrooms.

Process

Skilled discussion as a process requires mindfulness about focusing on one topic and applying one process tool at a time. When topics and processes blur group members lose focus. To maintain focus requires clear structure, purposeful facilitation, impulse control on the part of individual group members and recovery strategies if the group strays off course.

Effective group members share responsibility with the facilitator for maintaining the flow of the discussion, for encouraging other group members to share knowledge, and ideas, for hearing and exposing points of confusion or murkiness.

When working groups stray from skilled discussion, they often move to an unskilled form of debate. This occurs when group members overlook the useful advocacy of ideas and proposals and start listening for and challenging the fallacies in the arguments of others. *Battuere,* the Latin origin of the word debate, means to "fight or beat down." When meetings descend to the level of street debate, rather academic debate, we focus on beating down the ideas of others. Scoring points becomes the goal and winning comes from intimidation and intonation as much as from --- or more than---logic or reason.

The Adaptive School: Developing and Facilitating Collaborative Groups . Center for Adaptive Schools . www.adaptive-schools.com

37

Details

Whereas successful dialogue requires attention to the whole, successful discussion focuses on the details, both in isolation and in their interactions. The path of discussion is also the path of decision. As such, groups need to identify any constraints under which they might be working such as, timelines, deadlines, budgets, product standards, the negotiable items, the nonnegotiable items, task assignments ,and, most important who they are in the decision-making process.

Groups that are skilled in discussion employ many intentional cognitive skills. There is no set sequence for these efforts. The task before the group determines the necessary intellectual toolkit.

Groups need tools for the following:

• Generating ideas, including a repertoire of brainstorming and creative thinking strategies and protocols

• Organizing ideas, including both conceptual and graphic tools

• Analyzing ideas, including a variety of tools for exposing assumptions and clarifying particulars

• Deciding among alternatives, including the clarification of decision-making roles and processes

Decision as the Outcome

Decision, in its Latin root *decidere,* means "to cut off or determine." In practice this means to cut off some choices. The purpose of discussion is to eliminate some ideas from a field of possibilities and allow the stronger ideas to prevail. Groups must learn to separate people from ideas in order for this to work effectively. If ideas are "owned" by individuals, then to cut the idea away is the same as cutting the person away. Ideas once stated should belong to the group, not to individuals. In this way they can be shaped, modified, and discarded to serve the group's greater purposes.

Professional Community

Professional community is both a cause and an effect of the two ways of talking. As a cause, being in a community provides the motivation and vision of ways of interacting and working together. As an effect, a strong professional community results from both what is talked about and how people talk. Such talk requires courage, confidence in self and others and skillfulness in applying the maps and tools for developing shared understanding and strategic decision-making practices.

The Adaptive School: Developing and Facilitating Collaborative Groups . Center for Adaptive Schools . www.adaptive-schools.com

38

The Adaptive School: Developing and Facilitating Collaborative Groups . Center for Adaptive Schools . www.adaptive-schools.com

39

Seven Norms of Collaboration

When spider webs unite, they can tie up a lion.
Egyptian proverb

The Adaptive School: Developing and Facilitating Collaborative Groups . Center for Adaptive Schools . www.adaptive-schools.com

41

Promoting a Spirit of Inquiry

We can make our world significant by the courage of our questions and the depth of our answers.

----Carl Sagan

High-functioning groups and group members infuse their work with a spirit of inquiry. Inquiry is central to professional communities that produce stable gains in student learning. Learning at its roots is a questioning process and successful collaboration embraces the patterns and practices of inquiry. Inquiry presumes an openness to and an investment in the ideas of others. The Physicist, David Bohm, has noted that thought is "largely a collective phenomenon." These thoughts like electrons are shaped by their interactions with others. (Senge, 1990).

To inquire is to ask, be curious, invite the transmission of thoughts or feelings, confer, consult, wonder, request, examine and investigate ideas. Richard Elmore (2000) notes that "…the knowledge we need to solve problems (in schools) often doesn't reside close at hand; it has to be found through active inquiry and analysis" (p. 13) Such interactions are not always the norm in schools. Collaborative work is fraught with the tensions and the fears of being judged or of being perceived as one who might be judging others.

Teaching as a private practice has a deep cultural history. Breaking and reshaping the patterns within a culture requires both skill and commitment to the ongoing process of building community. Teaching is in many ways a telling profession. Teachers tell students what they need to know and how to do the things they need to learn how to do. This telling behavior often carries over into patterns of adult communication as we tell others our stories, thoughts and opinions or wait for our turn to do so. This culture of advocacy defines much of the interaction in adult groups. We are often caught up in the tyranny of *or* (Collins & Porras, 1997). Things must be either right or wrong, true or false, yes or no.

Dichotomous thinking leads to dichotomous questions, which in turn polarize group members. The art of asking invitational questions that avoid these dichotomies is the heart of collaborative inquiry. Invitational questions form connections between people and ideas as well as between ideas and other ideas.

All group work is about relationships. Relationships shape and define patterns of discourse. These relationships are shaped by who initiates a query and the form of that query. Who responds and how he or she respond is a direct result of the ways in which a topic is initiated. Form, function and outcome are linked within an emotional and social system that when handled with care opens and expands thought and creates new possibilities.

The patterns of inquiry built with the tools of the seven norms lead to deeper understanding and to

The Adaptive School: Developing and Facilitating Collaborative Groups . Center for Adaptive Schools . www.adaptive-schools.com

42

better-informed action. This understanding and these actions can be internal for participants and external in their behaviors. As we grapple with ideas and perspectives, we come to know others and ourselves more deeply. To do so requires us to reflect on our inner and outer reactions to data, information and events. Purposeful inquiry helps us to interpret personal and collective values and the implications of these as we live them out in our organizations. Skillful inquiry also helps us to clarify our priorities for a topic on the table. Where does this issue fit within the bigger picture? In what ways is this topic important and in what ways might this topic be a distraction?

In the end, what we talk about and how we talk to one another is a way of acting out our beliefs about the world and the way it works, our beliefs about the group and its purposes and our beliefs about our personal place in both arenas. What we talk about and how we talk also defines who we are and ultimately whom we become. By promoting a spirit of inquiry within our groups, we make an investment in our personal and collective futures.

The Adaptive School: Developing and Facilitating Collaborative Groups . Center for Adaptive Schools . www.adaptive-schools.com

43

The Seven Norms of Collaborative Work

Pausing: Pausing before responding or asking a question allows time for thinking and enhances dialogue, discussion and decision-making.

Paraphrasing: Using a paraphrase starter that is comfortable for you "So..." or "As you are..." or "You're thinking..." and following the starter with a paraphrase assists members of the group to hear and understand one another as they formulate decisions.

Putting inquiry at the center: Inquiring to explore perceptions, assumptions and interpretations and inviting others to inquire into their own thinking. Inquiring into the ideas of others' before advocating for one's own ideas.

Probing: Using gentle open-ended probes or inquiries such as, "Please say more..." or "I'm curious about..." or "I'd like to hear more about..." or "Then, are you saying...?" increases the clarity and precision of the group's thinking.

Placing ideas on the table: Ideas are the heart of a meaningful dialogue. Label the intention of your comments. For example, you might say, "Here is one idea..." or "One thought I have is..." or "Here is a possible approach...".

Paying attention to self and others: Meaningful dialogue is facilitated when each group member is conscious of self and of others and is aware of not only what he or she is saying, but also how it is said and how others are responding. This includes paying attention to learning style when planning for, facilitating and participating in group meetings. Responding to others in their own language forms is one manifestation of this norm.

Presuming positive intentions: Assuming that others' intentions are positive promotes and facilitates meaningful dialogue and eliminates unintentional putdowns. Using positive intentions in your speech is one manifestation of this norm.

The Adaptive School: Developing and Facilitating Collaborative Groups . Center for Adaptive Schools . www.adaptive-schools.com

45

Norms Inventory - Rating Perceptions of Myself

Pausing to allow time for thought

1. I pause after asking questions.

Low _____/_____/_____/_____ High

2. I pause after others speak to reflect before responding.

Low _____/_____/_____/_____ High

3. I pause before asking questions to allow time for artful construction.

Low _____/_____/_____/_____ High

Paraphrasing within a pattern of pause - paraphrase - question to ensure deep listening

1. I listen and paraphrase to acknowledge and clarify.

Low _____/_____/_____/_____ High

2. I listen and paraphrase to summarize and organize.

Low _____/_____/_____/_____ High

3. I listen and paraphrase to shift levels of abstraction.

Low _____/_____/_____/_____ High

Putting inquiry at the center to reveal and extend thinking

1. I inquire to explore perceptions, assumptions and interpretations.

Low _____/_____/_____/_____ High

2. I invite others to inquire into my perceptions, assumptions and interpretations.

Low _____/_____/_____/_____ High

3. I inquire before I advocate.

Low _____/_____/_____/_____ High

The Adaptive School: Developing and Facilitating Collaborative Groups . Center for Adaptive Schools . www.adaptive-schools.com

46

Probing to clarify

1. I seek understanding of the meaning of words.

Low _____/_____/_____/_____ High

2. I seek understanding of data, explanations, ideas, anecdotes and generalizations.

Low _____/_____/_____/_____ High

3. I seek understanding of assumptions, perceptions and interpretations.

Low _____/_____/_____/_____ High

Placing ideas on the table and pulling them off / placing data and perceptions before the group

1. I state the intentions of my communications.

Low _____/_____/_____/_____ High

2. I provide relevant facts, ideas, opinions and inferences.

Low _____/_____/_____/_____ High

3. I remove or announce modification of ideas, opinions and points of view.

Low _____/_____/_____/_____ High

Paying attention to self and others to monitor our ways of working

1. I balance participation and open opportunities for others to contribute and respond.

Low _____/_____/_____/_____ High

2. I restrain my impulses to react, respond or rebut at inappropriate times or in ineffective ways.

Low _____/_____/_____/_____ High

3. I maintain awareness of the group's task, processes and development.

Low _____/_____/_____/_____ High

Presuming positive intentions to support a nonjudgmental atmosphere

1. I communicate respectfully whether I agree or disagree.

Low _____/_____/_____/_____ High

2. I embed positive presuppositions in my paraphrases, summaries and comments.

Low _____/_____/_____/_____ High

3. I embed positive presuppositions when I inquire or probe for specificity.

Low _____/_____/_____/_____ High

The Adaptive School: Developing and Facilitating Collaborative Groups . Center for Adaptive Schools . www.adaptive-schools.com

47

Norms Inventory - Rating Our Perceptions of Our Group

Pausing to allow time for thought

1. We pause after asking questions.

Low _____/_____/_____/_____ High

2. We pause after others speak to reflect before responding.

Low _____/_____/_____/_____ High

3. We pause before asking questions to allow time for artful construction.

Low _____/_____/_____/_____ High

Paraphrasing within a pattern of pause - paraphrase - question to ensure deep listening

1. We listen and paraphrase to acknowledge and clarify.

Low _____/_____/_____/_____ High

2. We listen and paraphrase to summarize and organize.

Low _____/_____/_____/_____ High

3. We listen and paraphrase to shift levels of abstraction.

Low _____/_____/_____/_____ High

Putting inquiry at the center to reveal and extend thinking

1. We inquire to explore perceptions, assumptions and interpretations.

Low _____/_____/_____/_____ High

2. We invite others to inquire into our perceptions, assumptions and interpretations.

Low _____/_____/_____/_____ High

3. We inquire before we advocate.

Low _____/_____/_____/_____ High

The Adaptive School: Developing and Facilitating Collaborative Groups . Center for Adaptive Schools . www.adaptive-schools.com

48

Probing to clarify

1. We seek understanding of the meaning of words.

Low _____/_____/_____/_____ High

2. We seek understanding of data, explanations, ideas, anecdotes and generalizations.

Low _____/_____/_____/_____ High

3. We seek understanding of assumptions, perceptions and interpretations.

Low _____/_____/_____/_____ High

Placing ideas on the table and pulling them off / placing data and perceptions before the group

1. We state the intentions of our communications.

Low _____/_____/_____/_____ High

2. We provide relevant facts, ideas, opinions and inferences.

Low _____/_____/_____/_____ High

3. We remove or announce modification of ideas, opinions and points of view.

Low _____/_____/_____/_____ High

Paying attention to self and others to monitor our ways of working

1. We balance participation and open opportunities for each other to contribute and respond.

Low _____/_____/_____/_____ High

2. We restrain our impulses to react, respond or rebut at inappropriate times or in ineffective ways.

Low _____/_____/_____/_____ High

3. We maintain awareness of the group's task, processes and development.

Low _____/_____/_____/_____ High

Presuming positive intentions to support a non-judgmental atmosphere

1. We communicate respectfully whether we agree or disagree.

Low _____/_____/_____/_____ High

2. We embed positive presuppositions in our paraphrases, summaries and comments.

Low _____/_____/_____/_____ High

3. We embed positive presuppositions when we inquire or probe for specificity.

The Adaptive School: Developing and Facilitating Collaborative Groups . Center for Adaptive Schools . www.adaptive-schools.com

49

Personal Seven Norms Assessment

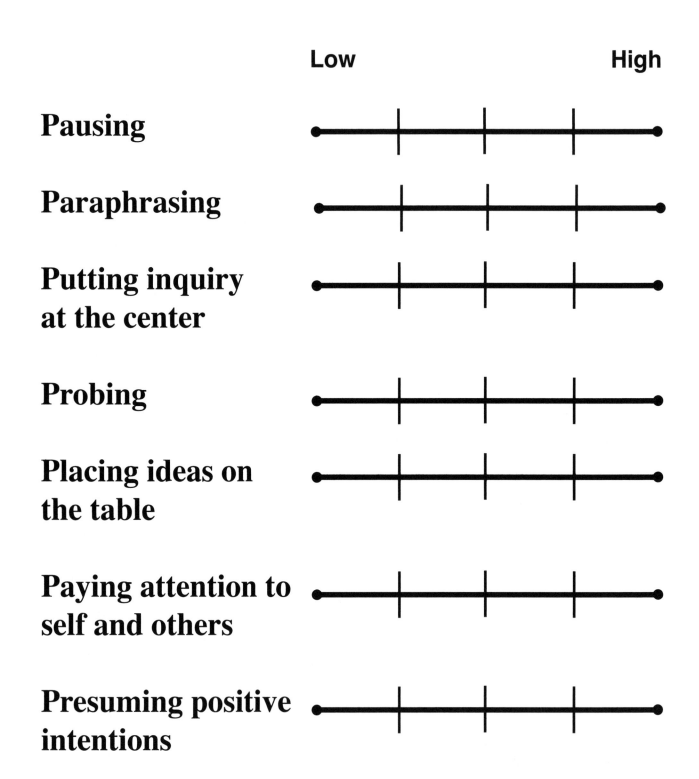

Low   High

Pausing

Paraphrasing

Putting inquiry
at the center

Probing

Placing ideas on
the table

Paying attention to
self and others

Presuming positive
intentions

The Adaptive School: Developing and Facilitating Collaborative Groups . Center for Adaptive Schools . www.adaptive-schools.com

50

Group Seven Norms Assessment

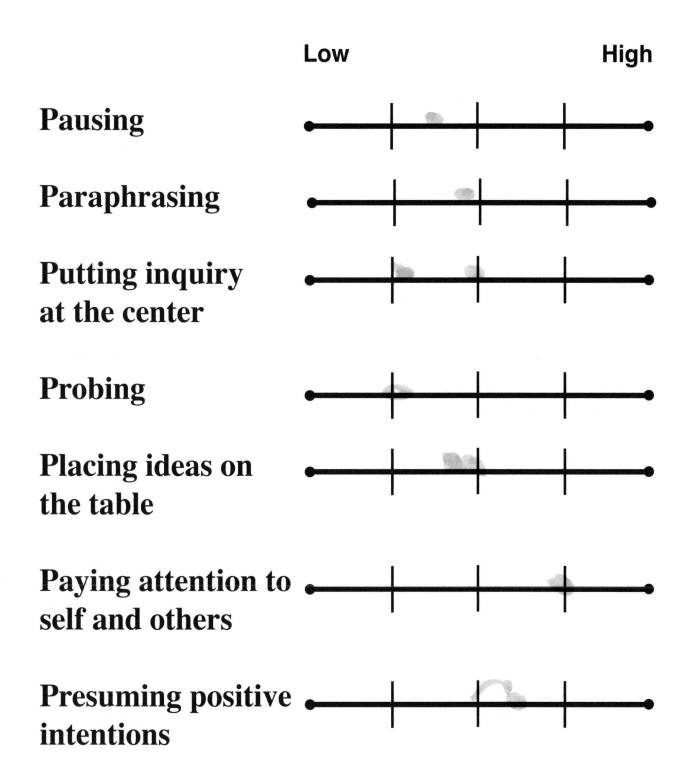

The Adaptive School: Developing and Facilitating Collaborative Groups . Center for Adaptive Schools . www.adaptive-schools.com

51

Pausing

There is a vast research base on the positive effects of teacher pausing and silence on student thinking. The "wait time" research of Mary Budd Rowe (1986) has been replicated around the world. Thinking takes time. High-level thinking takes even longer. This research indicates that it takes from 3 to 5 seconds for most human brains to process high-level thoughts.

Not all brains work the same way. This is especially evident in meetings and group work. Some people prefer to think out loud and construct their ideas externally; others prefer to process ideas internally and reflect and analyze before speaking. The external processors often get in the way of the internal processors. This can be an alienating experience for deliberate, internal thinkers. The meeting topics move by before they have had a chance to contribute.

Groups become skilled at four types of pauses. The first type occurs after a question is asked. This allows initial processing time for those being asked the question. The second type occurs after someone speaks. Human beings think and speak in bursts. With additional processing time, more thoughts are organized into coherent speech.

The first two types of pauses require the questioner and other group members to monitor and control their own behavior. These are pauses to give other people time to think. A third type is under the control of each individual who is asked a question. This is personal reflection time in which that person waits before answering. Sometimes one says, "Give me a moment to think about that before answering." At other times one acknowledges the question nonverbally, goes inside oneself to think, and then responds to the question. This is also a nice way to model thoughtfulness for others and can be an important normative behavior in groups.

A fourth type of pause in meetings is a collective pause. This can be formally structured or can occur spontaneously. These shared pauses allow ideas and questions to settle in and allow time for note taking and reflection. The intent of these breaks in the action is to create shared cognitive space for the group and its members.

Pausing begins a pattern that is followed by paraphrasing and questioning. Groups give themselves a powerful gift when they establish this pattern as a norm; pause, paraphrase, and probe for details; pause, paraphrase, and inquire for a wider range of thoughts; and pause, paraphrase, and inquire about feelings.

Wait Time I	Wait Time II	Wait Time III
Pause after asking a question to: • allow thinking time • signal support for thinking • demonstrate your belief in the capacities of others for thinking	Pause after group members respond to: • allow time for retrieval of additional or related information • encourage piggybacking of ideas	Pause before your own responses or additional questions to: • model thoughtfulness • signal your need to think before responding

The Adaptive School: Developing and Facilitating Collaborative Groups . Center for Adaptive Schools . www.adaptive-schools.com

52

Paraphrasing

Paraphrasing is one of the most valuable and least used communication tools in meetings. Even people who naturally and skillfully paraphrase in one-to-one settings often neglect this vital behavior in group settings. Groups that develop consciousness about paraphrasing and give themselves permission to use this reflected tool become clearer and more cohesive about their work.

There are three broad categories of paraphase types:
1. Acknowledge and clarify content and emotion. If the paraphrase is not completely accurate, the speaker will offer corrections. "So you're concerned about the budgeting process and ways to get input early."

2. Summarize and organize by offering themes and "containers" to organize several statements or separate jumbled issues. This is an especially important type of paraphrase to use when multiple speakers contribute to a topic. "There appear to be two issues here. One is resource allocation and the other is the impact of those decisions on student learning."

3. Shift to a higher or lower level of abstraction. Paraphrasing within a flow of discourse often moves through a sequence of acknowledging, summarizing, and shifting the focus to a higher or lower level of abstraction. Paraphrases move to a higher abstractional level when they name concepts, goals, values, and assumptions: "So a major goal here is to define fairness in the budgeting processes and compare those criteria to the operating values of the school." Paraphrases move to a lower abstractional level when concepts require grounding in details: "So fair might mean that we construct a needs assessment form for each department to fill out and submit to the site council for public consideration."

Three Types of Paraphrasing

Acknowledge/Clarify	Summarize/Organize	Shift Level of Abstraction	
a brief statement in the listener's own words.	a statement that offers themes or containers	a statement that shifts the conversation to a higher or lower level of abstraction	
Metaphorically: a mirror	Metaphorically: baskets /boxes	Metaphorically: elevator/ escalator	
• You're concerned about.... • You would like to see.... • You're feeling badly about....	• You seem to have two goals here: one is about ____ and the other is about _____. • We seem to be struggling with three themes: where to ___, how to _____, and who should_____. • On the one hand we _____ and on the other we_____.	**Shifting up:** • value • belief • goal • assumption • concept • category • intention	**Shifting down:** • example • nonexample • strategy • choice • action • option • possibility

The Adaptive School: Developing and Facilitating Collaborative Groups . Center for Adaptive Schools . www.adaptive-schools.com

53

Putting Inquiry at the Center

Thinking is a biochemi[...] [obscured] [...]tion and the molecules of cognition. We are wirec [...] [obscured] [...]ners. Reducing the potential for threat in our questions n[...] [obscured] [...]he topic of our inquiry. To keep others open and thinkin[...] [obscured] [...]t features in our communication.

Handwritten note:
The → some
could → might
is → seems
why → what

Full Attention
The invitation to think b[...] [obscured] [...] signaling that our full presence is available for this conver[...] [obscured] [...]ical message meshes with several important verbal elemen[...] [obscured] [...] think about the ideas being explored.

Approachable Voice
Using an approachable v[...] [obscured] [...] voice is well modulated and tends to rise at the end of [...] [obscured] (Grinder 1997). This tonal package wraps around our questions and comments indicating the intention to invite and explore thinking and not to interrogate or challenge.

Plural Forms
Two important syntactical choices invite colleagues to think with us and increase the options and possibilities for thinking. The first is to use plural forms; *observations* instead of *observation*, *options* instead of *option*. The use of plural forms sets aside the need for evaluation and the sorting of ideas. Often group members need to hear their ideas aloud before they know which are most central to the issues before the group.

Exploratory Language
The second syntactical element is the use of exploratory phrasing in statements, paraphrases and questions. Words like *some*, *might*, *seems*, *possible*, and *hunches* widen the potential range of responses and reduce the need of confidence and surety. Words like *could* and *why* may decrease the confidence of listeners by seeming to ask for premature commitment or a need to defend ideas and actions that are not yet fully developed.

Nondichotomous Questions
Invitational and mediational facilitators and group members frame their questions using the elements listed above. In addition, they frame their questions by using open-ended, nondichotomous forms. These are questions that cannot be answered yes or no. For example, instead of asking a group, "Did anyone notice anything unusual in this data set?" they ask, "What are some interesting our unusual things that you noticed in this data set?" By eliminating dichotomous stems such as, "Can you," "Did you," "Will you," or "Have you," facilitators and skilled group members invite productive thinking and promote a spirit of inquiry within the group.

Adapted with permission from: B. Wellman & L. Lipton, (2004). Data-Driven Dialogue: A Facilitator's Guide to Collaborative Inquiry. Sherman, CT: MiraVia LLC.

The Adaptive School: Developing and Facilitating Collaborative Groups . Center for Adaptive Schools . www.adaptive-schools.com

54

Probing to Clarify

Facilitators and facilitative group members ask questions to elicit or clarify deleted, distorted or overgeneralized statements. They ask clarifying questions to construct shared understanding and to increase the meaning of what others are saying. Pausing and paraphrasing should precede the probe for specificity.

Five fundamental categories of communication might require probing for specificity.

Nouns and Pronouns *the students, the parents, the administrators, the textbooks, the district, they, others, people....*

To respond: pause, paraphrase and inquire, *"Which students specifically?"*

Verbs *think, do, feel, plan, engage, study, learn, observe, improve, enhance...*

To respond: pause, paraphrase and inquire, *"Think how specifically?"*

Comparators *better, larger, smarter, slower, more profound, less important....*

To respond: pause, paraphrase and inquire, *"Better in which ways?"*

Rule Words *can't, shouldn't, must, have to, ought to.....*

To respond: pause, paraphrase and inquire, *"What would happen if you did?"*

"What would happen if you didn't?" *"Who made up that rule?"*

Universal Quantifiers *everyone, all, no one, always, never*

To respond: pause, paraphrase and inquire, *"Everyone?"*
"Can you think of someone who does not?
"Do you mean everyone in North America?"

The Adaptive School: Developing and Facilitating Collaborative Groups . Center for Adaptive Schools . www.adaptive-schools.com

55

Placing Ideas on the Table

Ideas are the heart of group work. In order to be effective, they must be released to the group. "Here is an idea for consideration. One possible approach to this issue might be . . . " When ideas are owned by individuals, the other group members tend to interact with the speaker out of their feelings for and relationship to the speaker rather than with the ideas presented. This is especially true when the speakers have role or knowledge authority related to the topic at hand. To have an idea be received in the spirit in which you tell it, label your intentions: "This is one idea" or "Here is a thought" or "This is not an advocacy, I am just thinking out loud."

Knowing when to pull ideas off the table is equally important. "I think this idea is blocking us; let's set it aside and move on to other possibilities." In this case, continued advocacy of the idea is not influencing other group members' thinking. This is a signal to pull back and reconsider approaches.

Productive group work is driven by data, both qualitative and quantitative. Data about student learning, school climate, teacher satisfaction, parent satisfaction, and the like are important grounded ideas to put on the table. Collaborative work in schools requires data as well as impressions. In fact, important learning is possible whether or not the data align with the impressions of group members.

Paying Attention to Self and Others

Meaningful dialogue and discussion is facilitated when each group member is conscious of oneself and of others. Skilled group members are aware of what they are saying, how they are saying it, and how others are receiving and responding to their ideas. This includes paying attention to both physical and verbal cues in oneself and others. Since the greatest part of communication occurs nonverbally, group members need consciousness about their total communication package (Goleman, 2006). This includes posture, gesture, proximity, muscle tension, facial expression, and the pitch, pace, volume, and inflection in their voices.

One important skill to develop is paying attention to and responding to the learning styles of others. The earlier section on paraphrasing offers some tips for communicating with global and concrete thinkers. In addition to using those ideas, skilled group members should try to match the language forms of others. This occurs when the respondent joins in a metaphor offered by another. It also occurs when the respondent matches the representation system of the speaker by using visual, kinesthetic, or auditory words in response to hearing the speaker operate within one or more of those categories (Lankton, 1980). Here's an example:

Speaker: "I'd like to see us develop a workable action plan."

Respondent: "So you have an image of a practical process that we can apply to our work. What are some of the features you'd like to have on view before us?"

The Adaptive School: Developing and Facilitating Collaborative Groups . Center for Adaptive Schools . www.adaptive-schools.com

56

Presuming Positive Intentions

Assuming that others' intentions are positive encourages honest conversations about important matters. This is an operating stance that group members must take if dialogue and discussion are to flourish; it is also a linguistic act for speakers to frame their paraphrases and inquiries within positive presuppositions.

Positive presuppositions reduce the possibility of the listener perceiving threats or challenges in a paraphrase or question. Instead of asking, "Does anybody here know why these kids aren't learning?" the skilled group member might say, "Given our shared concern about student achievement, I'd like to examine our assumptions about what might be causing gaps in learning."

The first question is likely to trigger defensiveness. The second approach will most likely lead to speculation, exploration, and collective understanding. This is especially true when a speaker has strong emotions about a topic and even more important when the respondent initially disagrees with the speaker. Here's an example:

Speaker: "I'm really ticked off about the lack of communication in this school. We never find out about the important things until everyone else knows about them. In fact, I get more district news from the local paper than I do from internal sources."
Respondent: "So as a committed professional, you'd like useful information about our organization in a timely fashion and in a means convenient for you. As you think about such a system, what might be some important components?"

In the example above the respondent presumes that the speaker is a committed professional who wants to solve a real problem. People tend to act as if such presuppositions are true. The emotional processors in the brain hear the positive intention and open up access to high-level thinking (Ledoux, 1996).

Name Those Presuppositions

• A skillful group wouldn't always get defensive and confused.

• Even this group should be able to solve that problem.

• Thanks for sharing. Does anyone have a constructive idea?

• Can we hear some practical suggestions now?

• If the subcommittee had listened to us, we wouldn't be talking about this now.

• A caring facilitator would have let that happen.

The Adaptive School: Developing and Facilitating Collaborative Groups . Center for Adaptive Schools . www.adaptive-schools.com

57

Inquiry

Invite others to make their thinking visible --creating psychological safety

• **Attend fully-** by being physically and emotionally present with others.

• **Use an approachable voice -** tonal quality signals our intention to inquire, not interrogate.

• **Use plural forms -** plurals open the questions, producing more than one possible appropriate answer.

• **Use exploratory language -** to qualify your questions and make them "safer" to answer. "What are some of ... How might you... What are your hunches about...?"

• **Use nondichotomous questions -** these are questions that cannot be answered "yes" or "no" or "true" or "false".

• **Use positive presuppositions -** these language forms assume capacity and positive intentions. "Given your knowlege of....", As an experienced professional...."

• **Use a pattern of pausing, paraphrasing, pausing again before inquiring or probing for specificity.**

Inquire for the elements of the advocacy template that the speaker has not yet illuminated.

• **Describe the focus of your advocacy.** "What are some of your assumptions about this issue?

• **Describe your reasoning.** "Given your concern and knowledge of this issue, what are some of the observations and data that are influencing you?"

• **Describe your feelings.** "What are some of your feelings about this issue?"

• **Distinguish data from interpretation.** "Help us to understand some of your interpretation of the data?"

• **Reveal your perspective.** "What are some of the perspectives you are considering as you reflect on this issue?"

• **Frame the wider context that surrounds this issue.** "As you consider the bigger picture, what are some of the factors and possible ripple effects that might be involved?"

• **Give concrete examples.** "What are some examples that occur to you about how this might play out?'

The Adaptive School: Developing and Facilitating Collaborative Groups . Center for Adaptive Schools . www.adaptive-schools.com

58

Advocacy

Make your thinking and reasoning visible

Describe the focus of your advocacy. "An issue that is important to me is..." "My assumptions are..."

Describe your reasoning. "I came to this conclusion because..."

Describe your feelings. "I feel _____ about this."

Distinguish data from interpretation. "This is the data I have as objectively as I can state it. Now here is what I think the data means."

Reveal your perspective. "I'm seeing this from the viewpoint of _____ or _____ or _____."

Frame the wider context that surrounds this issue. "Several groups would be affected by what I propose..."

Give concrete examples. "To get a clear picture, imagine that you are in school X..."

Test your assumptions and conclusions

Encourage others to explore your model, assumptions and data. "What do you think about what I just said? Do you see any flaws in my reasoning? What can you add?"

Reveal where you are least clear. "Here's one area you might help me think through..."

Stay open. Encourage others to provide different views: "Do you see it differently?"

Search for distortions, deletions and generalizations. "In what I've presented, do you believe I might have overgeneralized, or left out data or reported data incorrectly?"

Adapted from Senge, P., et al. (1994). *The fifth discipline fieldbook.* **New York: Doubleday.**

The Adaptive School: Developing and Facilitating Collaborative Groups . Center for Adaptive Schools . www.adaptive-schools.com

59

From Inquiry to Advocacy

Signal your intention to shift from inquiring to advocating

Gesture, posture, voice qualities and silence have contextual meaning based on the setting and verbal message. Mark your intentions to transition from inquiry to advocacy with some of these forms of paralanguage. For example:

• **Shift your body.** To signal a shift in the direction of the conversational energy.

• **Break eye contact.** To momentarily break rapport.

• **Pause.** To "gently interrupt" the speaker and refocus attention.

• **Employ a frozen gesture.** To nonverbally hold the pause.

• **Use an approachable voice.** To maintain psychological safety.

• **Use transition stems.** To relate your new thought to the flow of the conversation.

Use transition stems

"Here is a related thought..."

"I hold it another way..."

"Hmmm, from another perspective..."

"An additional idea might be..."

"An assumption I'm exploring is..."

"Taking that one step further..."

The Adaptive School: Developing and Facilitating Collaborative Groups . Center for Adaptive Schools . www.adaptive-schools.com

60

The Adaptive School: Developing and Facilitating Collaborative Groups . Center for Adaptive Schools . www.adaptive-schools.com

61

Discussion

Structures for Collaborative Decision Making

I never teach my pupils, I only attempt to provide the conditions in which they can learn.
Albert Einstein

The Adaptive School: Developing and Facilitating Collaborative Groups . Center for Adaptive Schools . www.adaptive-schools.com

63

Organizing Principles

1. Meeting success is influenced more by the collaborative norms of the group than by the knowledge and skills of the group's facilitator.

2. The power of the group to produce results is rooted in the quality of the relationships among the participants.

3. In high-performing groups the five energy sources are the self-organizing values for every group and every meeting.

Meeting Success Structures

1. Decide who decides.

2. Define the sandbox.

3. Develop standards.

4. Design the surround.

The Adaptive School: Developing and Facilitating Collaborative Groups . Center for Adaptive Schools . www.adaptive-schools.com

64

Decision Making

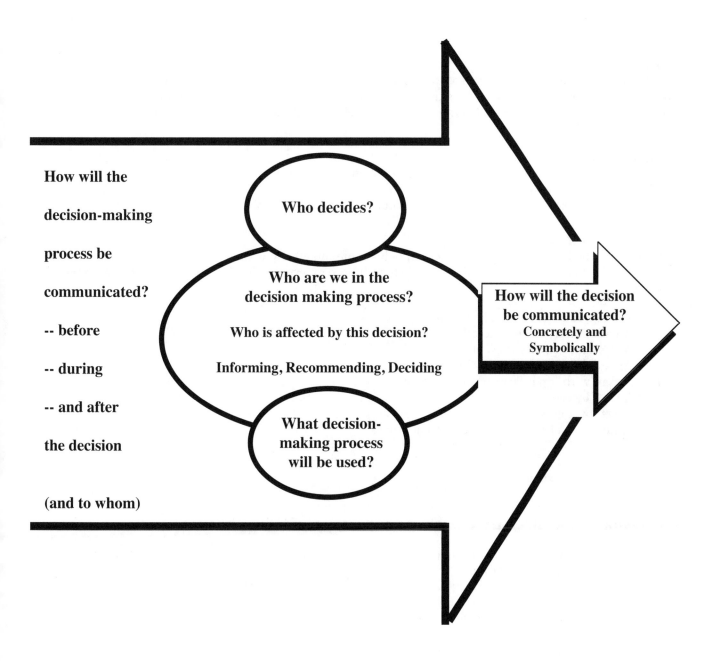

How will the
decision-making
process be
communicated?

-- before

-- during

-- and after

the decision

(and to whom)

Who decides?

Who are we in the
decision making process?

Who is affected by this decision?

Informing, Recommending, Deciding

What decision-
making process
will be used?

How will the decision
be communicated?
Concretely and
Symbolically

The Adaptive School: Developing and Facilitating Collaborative Groups . Center for Adaptive Schools . www.adaptive-schools.com

65

Decide Who Decides

Clarity

Clarity about decision making is one of the most critical functions related to meeting success. Often group members are not clear about who is making the final decision and what decision-making process will be used. It is important that people trust the process. Decision-making processes will often include these elements:

1. Who decides?
2. Who are we in the decision-making process? (informing, recommending, deciding)
3. What decision-making process will be used?
4. When and how will the decision be communicated to those involved?

Level of Authority

Determining who is making any final decision helps group members to know how to proceed. They need to determine who to influence internally and who to influence externally. The following are some possible decision locators:

- An individual or group above you
- An administrator unilaterally
- An administrator with input
- An administrator and staff by consensus
- A staff with input from administrators
- A staff by consensus
- Astaff by a vote
- A subgroup of a staff with input from others
- A subgroup of a staff unilaterally
- Individual staff members, selecting from a menu of options
- Parents and community members
- Students

Clarify and Communicate the Decision and Implementation Process

- Identify and periodically examine the full impact and consequences of the decision. Communicate these to all parties involved.
- Involve all parties whose working conditions will be affected by the decision.
- Clarify the time line for deciding and implementing the decision.
- Decide. Then make an explicit statement of the decision or recommendations, summarizing all key points.
- Determine how and when the decision-making group will revisit the decision at a later date to evaluate or revise it if necessary. Commit to a reasonable time period for the decision to work.
- Close the loop. Communicate the reasons for the decision fully and clearly to all affected parties after the decision is made, including how people's input influenced the outcome.
- Plan how to monitor and support the day-to-day implementation of the decision and communicate these plans to everyone involved.
- Evaluate the decision and critique the process.

The Adaptive School: Developing and Facilitating Collaborative Groups . Center for Adaptive Schools . www.adaptive-schools.com

66

Define the Sandbox

- Decide Who Decides
- Define the Sandbox
- Develop Standards
- Design the Surround

Every group needs to be clear about which issues are within its sphere of responsibility and which lie outside its decision-making authority. Groups conserve precious energy by focusing resources where they have direct influence.

All groups have interests that intersect with other groups' decision-making authority. Collegial and political considerations must honor these overlapping areas of concern. Individual and collective vigilance in this area is an essential ingredient of group success.

Here are some examples of groups for which this structure is important:

• Departments
• Curriculum task forces
• School-improvement teams
• Ad hoc study or advisory groups
• Grade-level teams
• Student councils
• Faculties
• Parent-teacher groups

Here is an example of a school improvement team defining its sandbox:

• Conceptualize an annual plan for gathering and assessing data
• Provide data analysis support to teacher leaders
• Make program recommendations for professional development
• Serve as information conduit between administration and teachers
• Conduct meetings in the round to model
• Consult with bilingual advisory committee
• Consult with Title I parents
• Review student progress
• Review other data, such as parent involvement survey
• Recommend the number of staff-development days
• Review (annually) school discipline policy

The Adaptive School: Developing and Facilitating Collaborative Groups . Center for Adaptive Schools . www.adaptive-schools.com

67

The Unhappy Technology Committee

An elementary principal was under siege. The school technology committee, composed of parents and teachers, had written and received a technology grant from a community business partner. The initial elation at receiving the funding had been replaced by frustration.

The committee had submitted a list of desired equipment to the principal. The principal submitted the requisition for the equipment but was then contacted by the district technology coordinator, who informed the principal that that the desired equipment was not compatible with the District Master Technology Plan. The principal informed the committee. The committee was very upset. One of the parents involved who was knowledgeable about computers said that the district plan was totally outdated. The committee argued that since it had secured the funding it should be able to purchase the best equipment available for its students. The committee accused the principal of wasting time and ignoring its recommendations. The disagreement had escalated to a very unpleasant situation.

What are some of the possible underlying causes of the committee's unhappiness?

What are some of the things the principal could have done to avoid this problem?

Courtesy of Suzanne Riley

The Adaptive School: Developing and Facilitating Collaborative Groups . Center for Adaptive Schools . www.adaptive-schools.com

68

Consensus as the Holy Grail

Consensus is one form of decision making, but not the only form. Some groups get stuck trying to use consensus processes without a consciousness of the differences between dialogue and discussion.

There are two types of consensus: (a) opening consensus, which develops through dialogue, and (b) focusing consensus, which develops through discussion (Senge, 1990). Opening consensus means the consideration of perspectives and possibilities. Focusing consensus means winnowing choices by clarifying criteria and applying these criteria to the choices. Focusing consensus for complex issues depends upon effective opening consensus.

Ultimately, consensus is a value and belief system more than a decision-making process. Unless groups and group members are willing to hang out with the process for as long as it takes, they are not usually ready for full consensus decision making.

Work at the Center for Conflict Resolution points to the following necessary conditions for effective consensus decision making (Avery, Auvine, Streibel & Weiss, 1981).

1. Unity of purpose. There should be basic core agreements on what the group is about and how it operates.

2. Equal access to power. Consensus cannot work in formal hierarchies. Informal power also needs to be equally distributed.

3. Autonomy of the group for external hierarchical structures. It is very difficult for groups to use consensus processes if they are part of a larger organization that does not honor this way of making decisions.

4. Time. Consensus takes time and patience. Participants have to believe in the usefulness of this method enough to follow it and not the clock or calendar.

5. Attending to process. Group members must be willing to spend group time reflecting on process and modifying it as necessary.

The Adaptive School: Developing and Facilitating Collaborative Groups . Center for Adaptive Schools . www.adaptive-schools.com

69

6. Attending to attitudes. Group members must be willing to examine their own attitudes and be open to change. The key ingredients are trust and cooperation.

7. Willingness to learn and practice skills. Communication, meeting participation, and facilitation skills must be continually honed and refined to make consensus processes work.

Sufficient Consensus
Groups with whom we work are usually better served by sufficient consensus. This generally means that at least 80% of the group is willing to commit and to act. It also means that the others agree not to block or sabotage.

Sufficient consensus relies on both dialogue and discussion for its effectiveness. The norm of balancing advocacy and inquiry is essential. Any dissenting voices must be able to influence and persuade 80% of the group to carry the day. This also means that other group members can paraphrase and draw matters to a close if only a few voices line up on one side of an issue.

The Adaptive School: Developing and Facilitating Collaborative Groups . Center for Adaptive Schools . www.adaptive-schools.com

70

Develop Standards

- Decide Who Decides
- Define the Sandbox
- Develop Standards
- Design the Surround

- One process

- One topic

- Balance participation

- Engage cognitive conflict

- Understand and agree on roles

The Adaptive School: Developing and Facilitating Collaborative Groups . Center for Adaptive Schools . www.adaptive-schools.com

71

Four Possible Meeting Roles

- **Engaged participant**

- **Facilitator**

- **Recorder**

- **Person with role or knowledge authority**

The Adaptive School: Developing and Facilitating Collaborative Groups . Center for Adaptive Schools . www.adaptive-schools.com

72

Engaged Participant

- Uses seven norms of collaboration

- Monitors one's own and others' adherence to meeting standards

- Sets and tests working agreements

- Seeks and provides data

- Clarifies decision-making processes and levels of authority

- Opens the door for others to speak

- Tests consensus

- Listens to one's own listening

- Is conscious of one's own assumptions and knowledge and how these interfere with one's own listening

The Adaptive School: Developing and Facilitating Collaborative Groups . Center for Adaptive Schools . www.adaptive-schools.com

73

Facilitator

- Remains neutral to content

- Clarifies role with group

- Focuses group energy

- Keeps group on task

- Directs processes

- Encourages everyone to participate

- Protects participants and ideas from attack

- Contributes to agenda planning

- Elicits clarity regarding meeting follow-up

The Adaptive School: Developing and Facilitating Collaborative Groups . Center for Adaptive Schools . www.adaptive-schools.com

74

Recorder

- Remains neutral to content

- Supports facilitator

- Records basic ideas as the facilitator paraphrases them

- Keeps eyes on charts and not on group members

- Writes legibly using uppercase and lowercase printing

- Uses alternating colors to separate ideas

- Uses icons and simple graphics

- Keeps all charts visible to support group memory

The Adaptive School: Developing and Facilitating Collaborative Groups . Center for Adaptive Schools . www.adaptive-schools.com

75

Person With Role Authority

Before and After the Meeting

- Coordinates agenda design
- Develops group-member leadership
- Coordinates the activities of subcommittees
- Sees that meeting follow-through occurs
- Provides for evaluation

Person With Role or Knowledge Authority

During the Meeting

- Informs group about constraints and resources
- Advocates for own ideas
- Inquires about the ideas of others
- Actively participates

The Adaptive School: Developing and Facilitating Collaborative Groups . Center for Adaptive Schools . www.adaptive-schools.com

76

Design the Surround

• Decide Who Decides
• Define the Sandbox
• Develop Standards
• Design the Surround

In his book *Smart Schools* David Perkins (1992), describes the surround as the features around learners which by their very presence mediate thinking and behavior. Psychological, emotional, cognitive and physical elements contribute to the surround. Meeting designers and group developers give careful consideration to the following elements:

- **Physical space and room arrangement.** Specific tasks require conscious room arrangement and materials provisioning. The room arrangement both communicates and structures the desired interaction.

- **Task, norms and standards charts.** As reminders of task focus and working agreements, high-performing groups position charts that state outcomes for their tasks and charts that remind participants of collaborative norms, meeting standards and group-member capabilities.

- **Charting materials.** Group memory and graphic processes support learning and retention. Charting materials such as markers, tape, pads and easels should be readily available. Wall space also must be considered. Blank walls without other art work are best for meeting rooms. This lets each group craft the space to its own needs.

- **Emotional space.** People do not come to meetings as blank slates. They carry unfinished business from other aspects of their day and from previous meetings. Inclusion activities, such as a grounding, support people in becoming fully present both physically and emotionally. Group-member consciousness about the emotional surround is also enhanced through processing questions that address both thoughts and feelings.

The Adaptive School: Developing and Facilitating Collaborative Groups . Center for Adaptive Schools . www.adaptive-schools.com

77

Principles for Designing the Surround

1. All participants and the facilitator should be able to see and hear each other.

2. The seating arrangements should enable members to focus on the flip chart (or other writing devices) and the facilitator.

4. Seating arrangements should distinguish participants from nonparticipants.

5. Seating arrangements should accommodate movement, subgrouping with different partners and personal ownership of the entire room in contrast with identifying with a single chair or table.

6. Memory displays and public recording should support sound thinking about meeting content and processes.

The Adaptive School: Developing and Facilitating Collaborative Groups . Center for Adaptive Schools . www.adaptive-schools.com

78

Room Arrangement

Tips:

1. Face meeting away from doors.
2. Focus on easels, not one another.
3. Keep chairs close to avoid energy leaks.

Key:

R   Recorder
F   Facilitator
KA Knowledge Authority
RA Role Authority

Alternatives:

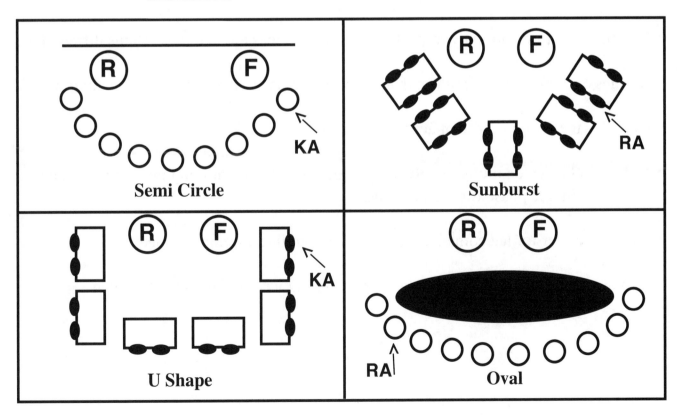

Semi Circle

Sunburst

U Shape

Oval

The Adaptive School: Developing and Facilitating Collaborative Groups . Center for Adaptive Schools . www.adaptive-schools.com

79

Benefits of Public Recording

• Helps the group focus on a task

• Supports visual learners

• Depersonalizes ideas and problem-bearing data

• Enhances memory of participants during and after the meeting

• Guards against data overload but holds on to all ideas; frees participants from taking notes

• Develops shared ownership

• Serves as a psychic release for participants

• Prevents repetititon and wheel spinning

• Encourages participation by respecting individual ideas and reducing status differentials

• Enables each member to confirm that his or her ideas are being recorded accurately

• Increases the group's sense of accomplishment

• Makes sophisticated problem-solving methods possible by holding on to information developed in one phase for use in the next

• Makes is easier for latecomers to catch up without interrupting the meeting

• Increases accountability by a public display noting *who* will do *what* by *when*

The Adaptive School: Developing and Facilitating Collaborative Groups . Center for Adaptive Schools . www.adaptive-schools.com

80

Tips for Public Recording

- **Materials**
  - Chart paper with 1 inch grid (27 x 34 inches)
  - Sturdy easels
  - Water color pens

- **Colors (2 or 3 only!)**
  - Earth colors for text and black for organizers (boxes, arrows, etc.)
  - Yellow or orange for highlighting
  - Red for titles only

- **Lettering**
  - At least 2 inches high
  - Print uppercase and lowercase
  - Consistent alphabet

- **Organizers**
  - Bullets in front of phrases
  - Lines between key lines
  - Box in parts of text

- **Graphic Assists**
  - Shaded borders
  - Simple pictographs
  - Numbered recording pages

- **Visual Thinking Maps**
  - List
  - Cluster
  - Matrix

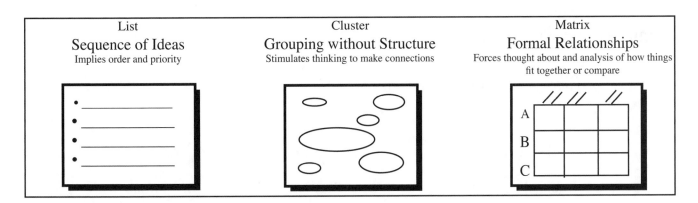

List	Cluster	Matrix
Sequence of Ideas	Grouping without Structure	Formal Relationships
Implies order and priority	Stimulates thinking to make connections	Forces thought about and analysis of how things fit together or compare

The Adaptive School: Developing and Facilitating Collaborative Groups . Center for Adaptive Schools . www.adaptive-schools.com

81

Meeting Inventory

Decide Who Decides

	Low	High

• We were clear about who we are in the decision making process.   1 - 2 - 3 - 4 - 5

• We were clear about the decision making processes being used.   1 - 2 - 3 - 4 - 5

Define the Sandbox

• We were clear about which parts of the issue(s) we explored live
  in our sandbox.   1 - 2 - 3 - 4 - 5

Develop Standards

• We adhered to one process at a time.   1 - 2 - 3 - 4 - 5

• We adhered to one topic at a time.   1 - 2 - 3 - 4 - 5

• We balanced participation.   1 - 2 - 3 - 4 - 5

  • The degree to which I felt listened to   1 - 2 - 3 - 4 - 5

  • The degree to which I listened to others   1 - 2 - 3 - 4 - 5

• We engaged in productive cognitive conflict.   1 - 2 - 3 - 4 - 5

• We were clear about meeting roles .   1 - 2 - 3 - 4 - 5

Design the Surround

• We managed the environment to support our work.   1 - 2 - 3 - 4 - 5

_____   _____   _____

Topic(s)   Date   Group

The Adaptive School: Developing and Facilitating Collaborative Groups . Center for Adaptive Schools . www.adaptive-schools.com

82

Meeting Organizer: Five Phases

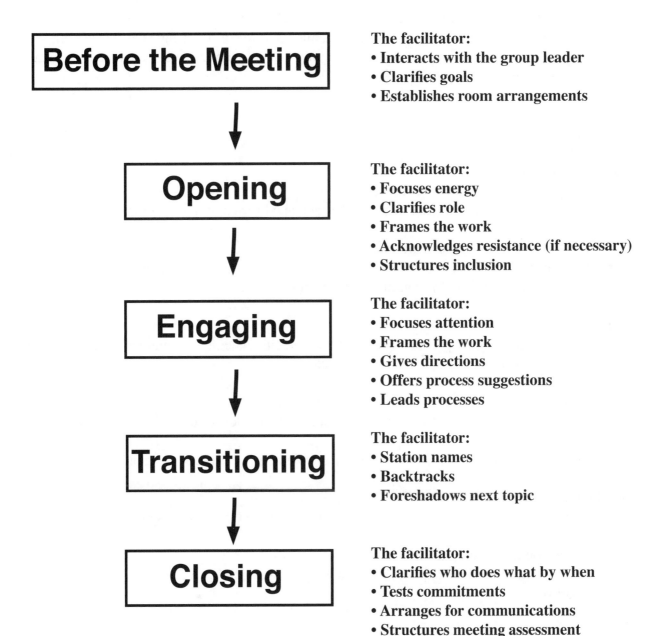

Before the Meeting

The facilitator:
- Interacts with the group leader
- Clarifies goals
- Establishes room arrangements

Opening

The facilitator:
- Focuses energy
- Clarifies role
- Frames the work
- Acknowledges resistance (if necessary)
- Structures inclusion

Engaging

The facilitator:
- Focuses attention
- Frames the work
- Gives directions
- Offers process suggestions
- Leads processes

Transitioning

The facilitator:
- Station names
- Backtracks
- Foreshadows next topic

Closing

The facilitator:
- Clarifies who does what by when
- Tests commitments
- Arranges for communications
- Structures meeting assessment
- Arranges for next meeting

The Adaptive School: Developing and Facilitating Collaborative Groups . Center for Adaptive Schools . www.adaptive-schools.com

83

Agenda Construction

Assuming that a group is doing reasonably well at maintaining the five standards for successful meeting - one content at a time, one process at a time, balanced participation, engaged cognitive conflict and agreement on meeting roles - the primary remaining challenge is to construct agendas that are organized for effectiveness and are not too long. This is the major problem many groups encounter in scheduled staff meetings and focused discussions.

Principles for Agenda Design

1. State clear outcomes
   - For the meeting and for each agenda item
   - State these behaviorally - list what will be seen and heard as evidence of success.

2. Separate reports and minutia from action items
   - Cluster reports and set a time limit for several - e.g., 5 reports, 15 minutes
   - Have reporters prepared to communicate the bottom line

3. Maximize member participation
   - Frequently engage subgroups - pairs, quartets, etc. in reflecting, generating ideas, responding to proposals, summarizing what occurred, etc.

4. Post public agendas
   - Visual processes are more effective than auditory strategies for directing group attention and energy
   - Show predicted times for discussing each agenda item, or clusters of, agenda items

5. Consider the emotions with which people may begin the meeting
   - Surface and address resistance, distress, and confusion at the beginning of the meeting

6. Structure reflection time about meeting processes
   - Use each meeting as an opportunity for a working group to learn from its experiences and improve

The Adaptive School: Developing and Facilitating Collaborative Groups . Center for Adaptive Schools . www.adaptive-schools.com

84

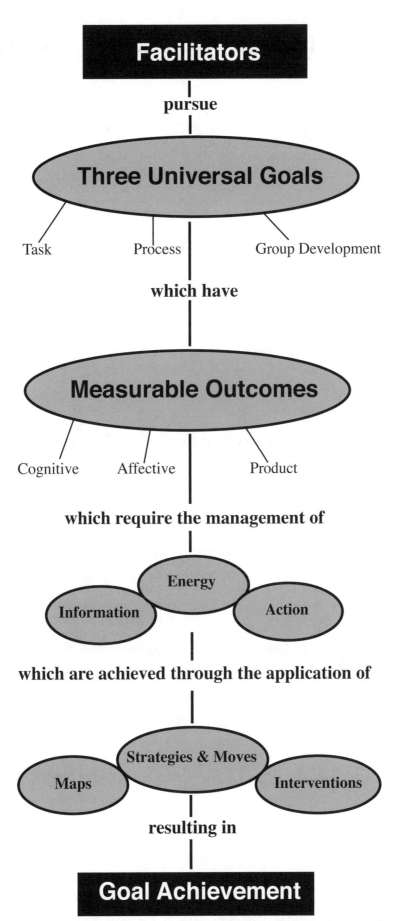

Facilitators

pursue

Three Universal Goals

Task   Process   Group Development

which have

Measurable Outcomes

Cognitive   Affective   Product

which require the management of

Energy

Information   Action

which are achieved through the application of

Strategies & Moves

Maps   Interventions

resulting in

Goal Achievement

The Adaptive School: Developing and Facilitating Collaborative Groups . Center for Adaptive Schools . www.adaptive-schools.com

85

Facilitator Self-Reflection

1. Who am I? About what do I care? How much do I dare?

2. Who is my client? The contact client -- an intermediate client -- a primary client -- an ultimate client?

3. What are my outcomes in this setting?

4. How is my expertise simultaneously an asset and a liability?

5. How can I distinguish between being right and being effective?

6. What lenses do I wear?

7. What types of capacities do I need to develop for this assignment?

The Adaptive School: Developing and Facilitating Collaborative Groups . Center for Adaptive Schools . www.adaptive-schools.com

86

Focusing Consensus Means

1. All participants contribute resources. Encourage use of one another's resources and opinions. View differences as helpful rather that as hinderances.

2. Everyone can paraphrase the issue.

3. Everyone has a chance to describe his or her feelings about the issue.

4. Those who continue to disagree indicate publicly that they are willing to go along for an experimental try for a prescribed period.

5. Everyone shares in the final decision.

Focusing Consensus Does Not Mean

1. There is a unanimous vote.

2. Everyone gets his or her first choice.

3. Everyone agrees. (A sufficient number must be in favor so the decision can be implemented successfully.)

The Adaptive School: Developing and Facilitating Collaborative Groups . Center for Adaptive Schools . www.adaptive-schools.com

87

Guidelines for Decision Making by Focusing Consensus

1. Avoid arguing for your own position.

2. Don't assume that someone must lose and someone must win at any point of stalemate. Seek the next most acceptable alternative.

3. Don't change your mind just to avoid a conflict.

4. Avoid attempts at conflict reduction, such as majority voting, averages, coin tosses, or bargaining.

The Adaptive School: Developing and Facilitating Collaborative Groups . Center for Adaptive Schools . www.adaptive-schools.com

88

Suggestions for Conducting a Focusing Four Consensus Activity

1. Explain each of the four steps before starting the activity.
2. Check for participant understanding.
3. Explain that the hand count or vote at the canvass stage will not make the decision of which options to recommend. The group will decide and be guided, not bound, by the data.
4. Begin the process.

Brainstorm

- Record brainstormed ideas on chart paper.
- Elicit ideas only.
- Discourage criticisms or questions.
- Push for 8-18 ideas.

Clarify

- Ask if any items should be clarified.
- The author of the idea provides clarification.
- The facilitator observes the questioner during the clarification and stops the clarification when the questioner indicates nonverbally or verbally that he or she understands.

Advocate

- Participants may advocate for as many items as they wish and as many times as they wish.
- Statements of advocacy must be phrased in the positive.
- Statements of advocacy must be brief.

Canvass

- Ask individuals in the group to identify which few ideas they feel are most important.
- To determine what a few is, use the formula: one-third plus one (If there are 12 items on the list, ask the group to identify 5 that are most important to them; if there are 15 items on the list, ask the group to identify 6.) They do not have to be placed in rank order.
- Take a hand count to determine which items are of greatest interest to the group.

The Adaptive School: Developing and Facilitating Collaborative Groups . Center for Adaptive Schools . www.adaptive-schools.com

89

The Focusing Four

• Brainstorm

and then

• Clarify

and then

• Advocate

and now

• Canvass

for a sense of the group's preferences

The Adaptive School: Developing and Facilitating Collaborative Groups . Center for Adaptive Schools . www.adaptive-schools.com

90

Tips for Using Focusing Four Consensus

1. Insist that all views be heard, understood and respected.

2. Legitimize all perceptions.

3. Confront problems, misunderstandings and bad feelings early in phases.

4. Address issues, not people.

5. Achieve agreement on the problem or the vision before going on to solutions.

6. Be explicit about each phase of problem solving.

7. Look for little successes first before tackling the big problem.

8. Look for ways of breaking fixation and redefining the problem/solution space. Avoid win/lose and either/or propositions.

9. Achieve agreement on the criteria before evaluating the alternatives.

10. Keep backing up to the phase and level of generality at which a foundation of agreements can be developed. Keep summing up the agreements.

11. Avoid premature motions.

12. Use formal voting as a last approach.

The Adaptive School: Developing and Facilitating Collaborative Groups . Center for Adaptive Schools . www.adaptive-schools.com

91

What to say when the group is running out of time

Ask the following questions:

- What is stopping us from making a decision?

- People seem disengaged. What's happening?

- Who would be willing to meet with Bernadine and Cirenio to develop this for the group to look at during the next meeting?

- Can we trust the subcommittee to make that decision?

- Would it be agreeable to the group if we asked Sam to bring us more information before we proceed?

- I think this is a decision for Savannah. Shall we ask her to make it?

The Adaptive School: Developing and Facilitating Collaborative Groups . Center for Adaptive Schools . www.adaptive-schools.com

92

Naive Questions

1. How much detail do we need to move this item?

2. Who is making this decision?

3. What is the process for making this decision?

4. What parts of this issue live in our sandbox?

5. Who will do what by when?

6. I'm trying to understand, is this a matter of principle or a matter of preference?

7. What conditions might cause us not to follow through on these agreements?

8. How will we know when we are successful?

9. Is there something we're not talking about that is keeping us stuck?

10. What questions would be useful to ask ourselves?

11. What are our assumptions about this?

The Adaptive School: Developing and Facilitating Collaborative Groups . Center for Adaptive Schools . www.adaptive-schools.com

93

Close Meetings With These Questions

1. Who will do what by when?

2. Who will communicate informally and formally to whom?

3. What will be communicated about the decisions of today's meeting?

4. What are the next steps?

5. Under what conditions would you be tempted to deviate from these communication agreements that we just made?

The Adaptive School: Developing and Facilitating Collaborative Groups . Center for Adaptive Schools . www.adaptive-schools.com

94

The Adaptive School: Developing and Facilitating Collaborative Groups . Center for Adaptive Schools . www.adaptive-schools.com

95

Working Effectively with Conflict

Conflict can be seen as a gift of energy, in which neither side loses and a new dance is created.

Thomas Crum

The Adaptive School: Developing and Facilitating Collaborative Groups . Center for Adaptive Schools . www.adaptive-schools.com

97

Outcomes of Conflict in Teams

Conflict can improve team effectiveness. The problem is that, once aroused, conflict is difficult to control. (Amason, et al, 1995, p. 29)

**C-Type Conflict
(Cognitive)**

Disagreements about substantive differences of opinion improve team effectiveness and produce:

- Better decisions
- Increased commitment
- Increased cohesiveness
- Increased empathy
- Increased understanding

**A-Type Conflict
(Affective)**

Disagreements over personalized, individually oriented matters reduce team effectiveness and produce:

- Destructive conflict
- Poorer decisions
- Decreased commitment
- Decreased cohesiveness

C-Type Conflict

As long as the disagreements among team members focus on substantive, issue-related differences of opinion, they tend to improve team effectiveness. Such cognitive conflict is a natural part of a properly functioning team. C-type conflict occurs as team members examine, compare and reconcile these differences. It requires teams to engage in activities that are essential to a team's effectiveness. It focuses attention on the all-too-often ignored assumptions that may underlie a particular issue.

A-Type Conflict

Affective conflict lowers team effectiveness by fostering hostility, distrust, cynicism, avoidance and apathy among team members. This type of conflict focuses on personalized anger or resentment, usually directed at specific individuals rather than ideas. It often emerges when C-type conflict becomes corrupted because members lack the skills or norms to disagree gracefully. In such settings, disagreement about ideas can become personalized.

Under these conditions, not only the quality of solutions declines, but also commitment to the team erodes because its members no longer identify themselves with the teams' actions. A downward spiral of reduced effectiveness results.

The Adaptive School: Developing and Facilitating Collaborative Groups . Center for Adaptive Schools . www.adaptive-schools.com

98

Teams that can use C-type conflict without generating A-type conflict develop abilities that other teams do not have.

Teams that encourage C without A achieve the following:

- **Focused activity**
  Effective teams work close to the core of issues and are not distracted by trivial points.

- **Creativity**
  Effective teams encourage thinking beyond normal options, listen to minority voices, encourage dissenting opinions, synergize the thoughts and perspectives of different members and approach problems from totally new perspectives.

- **Open communication**
  Conflict is an asset to maintaining open communications. Members in effective teams challenge one another's assumptions. Effective teams make the fullest possible use of all their members. In less effective groups there is often a disproportionate contribution between members. Good teams seek out the opinions of those who are less active and moderate the contribution of those who monopolize the conversation.

- **Integration**
  Effective teams have a work culture that allows members to speak freely and challenge the premises of other members' viewpoints without the threat of anger, resentment or retribution.

Adapted from Amason, Thompson, Hochwarter,, & Harrison (1995).

The Adaptive School: Developing and Facilitating Collaborative Groups . Center for Adaptive Schools . www.adaptive-schools.com

99

Seven Tips for Managing Yourself During Conflict

1. Remember that people (even you) are rarely as benevolent as they perceive themselves to be.

2. Remind yourself that others are rarely as evil as their opponents perceive them to be.

3. Be aware that people rarely spend as much time thinking about the issues as is assumed.

4. Realize that the behaviors of others are rarely planned or thought out. Most aspects of conflict spin off other events and are not the result of cold-hearted calculation.

5. Almost all behaviors are motivated by positive intention. These intentions frequently arise from people trying to take care of and protect themselves.

6. Previous patterns taint present perceptions. Every conflict has a history that extends beyond the present.

7. Go to the balcony and observe the interactions within the group whenever you have difficulty remembering any of the above.

The Adaptive School: Developing and Facilitating Collaborative Groups . Center for Adaptive Schools . www.adaptive-schools.com

100

Conflict and Community in Schools

1. "Schools are arenas of struggle, poorly coordinated and ideologically diverse, making conflict not cooperation the norm."

2. "Professional communities are often born in conflict because they demand substantial change in practice, challenge existing norms of privacy and autonomy, and question existing boundaries between cultures and power groups at school sites."

3. "Conflict is a critical factor in understanding what distinguishes a generic professional community of colleagues from a learning community engaged in ongoing inquiry and change."

Bette Achinstein, Conflict, Community and Diversity Among Schoolteachers

Leadership for Conflict

1. Develop forums for teachers to discuss differences.

2. Reinforce community values.

3. Demonstrate a willingness to live with ambiguity.

...Karen Seashore Louis and Sharon Kruse

4. Model critical self-exploration and vulnerability.

5. Foster openness to different perspectives.

6. Hand conflicts back to teachers and don't become the final authority.

7. Provide multiple structures, resources, professional development and practice in inquiry and shared decision making.

...Betty Achinstein

The Adaptive School: Developing and Facilitating Collaborative Groups . Center for Adaptive Schools . www.adaptive-schools.com

101

Exercises and Instruments

Finally you understand that the real motorcycle you're working on is you.

Robert M. Pirsig

The Adaptive School: Developing and Facilitating Collaborative Groups . Center for Adaptive Schools . www.adaptive-schools.com

103

Walk-About Review

NAME	NAME	NAME
NAME	NAME	NAME
NAME	NAME	NAME

The Adaptive School: Developing and Facilitating Collaborative Groups . Center for Adaptive Schools . www.adaptive-schools.com

104

Walk-About Review

Recollections		

Recollections

	NAME	NAME	NAME

Insights

	NAME	NAME	NAME

Applications

	NAME	NAME	NAME

The Adaptive School: Developing and Facilitating Collaborative Groups . Center for Adaptive Schools . www.adaptive-schools.com

105

Norms Inventory - Rating Perceptions of Myself

Pausing to allow time for thought

1. I pause after asking questions.

Low _____/_____/_____/_____ High

2. I pause after others speak to reflect before responding.

Low _____/_____/_____/_____ High

3. I pause before asking questions to allow time for artful construction.

Low _____/_____/_____/_____ High

Paraphrasing within a pattern of pause - paraphrase - question to ensure deep listening

1. I listen and paraphrase to acknowledge and clarify.

Low _____/_____/_____/_____ High

2. I listen and paraphrase to summarize and organize.

Low _____/_____/_____/_____ High

3. I listen and paraphrase to shift levels of abstraction.

Low _____/_____/_____/_____ High

Putting inquiry at the center to reveal and extend thinking

1. I inquire to explore perceptions, assumptions and interpretations.

Low _____/_____/_____/_____ High

2. I invite others to inquire into my perceptions, assumptions and interpretations.

Low _____/_____/_____/_____ High

3. I inquire before I advocate.

Low _____/_____/_____/_____ High

The Adaptive School: Developing and Facilitating Collaborative Groups . Center for Adaptive Schools . www.adaptive-schools.com

106

Probing to clarify

1. I seek understanding of the meaning of words.

Low _____/_____/_____/_____ High

2. I seek understanding of data, explanations, ideas, anecdotes and generalizations.

Low _____/_____/_____/_____ High

3. I seek understanding of assumptions, perceptions and interpretations.

Low _____/_____/_____/_____ High

Placing ideas on the table and pulling them off / placing data and perceptions before the group

1. I state the intentions of my communications.

Low _____/_____/_____/_____ High

2. I provide relevant facts, ideas, opinions and inferences.

Low _____/_____/_____/_____ High

3. I remove or announce modification of ideas, opinions and points of view.

Low _____/_____/_____/_____ High

Paying attention to self and others to monitor our ways of working

1. I balance participation and open opportunities for others to contribute and respond.

Low _____/_____/_____/_____ High

2. I restrain my impulses to react, respond or rebut at inappropriate times or in ineffective ways.

Low _____/_____/_____/_____ High

3. I maintain awareness of the group's task, processes and development.

Low _____/_____/_____/_____ High

Presuming positive intentions to support a non-judgmental atmosphere

1. I communicate respectfully whether I agree or disagree.

Low _____/_____/_____/_____ High

2. I embed positive presuppositions in my paraphrases, summaries and comments.

Low _____/_____/_____/_____ High

3. I embed positive presuppositions when I inquire or probe for specificity.

Low _____/_____/_____/_____ High

The Adaptive School: Developing and Facilitating Collaborative Groups . Center for Adaptive Schools . www.adaptive-schools.com

107

Norms Inventory - Rating Our Perceptions of Our Group

Pausing to allow time for thought

1. We pause after asking questions.

Low _____/_____/_____/_____ High

2. We pause after others speak to reflect before responding.

Low _____/_____/_____/_____ High

3. We pause before asking questions to allow time for artful construction.

Low _____/_____/_____/_____ High

Paraphrasing within a pattern of pause - paraphrase - question to ensure deep listening

1. We listen and paraphrase to acknowledge and clarify.

Low _____/_____/_____/_____ High

2. We listen and paraphrase to summarize and organize.

Low _____/_____/_____/_____ High

3. We listen and paraphrase to shift levels of abstraction.

Low _____/_____/_____/_____ High

Putting inquiry at the center to reveal and extend thinking

1. We inquire to explore perceptions, assumptions and interpretations.

Low _____/_____/_____/_____ High

2. We invite others to inquire into our perceptions, assumptions and interpretations.

Low _____/_____/_____/_____ High

3. We inquire before we advocate.

Low _____/_____/_____/_____ High

The Adaptive School: Developing and Facilitating Collaborative Groups . Center for Adaptive Schools . www.adaptive-schools.com

108

Probing to clarify

1. We seek understanding of the meaning of words.

Low _____/_____/_____/_____ High

2. We seek understanding of data, explanations, ideas, anecdotes and generalizations.

Low _____/_____/_____/_____ High

3. We seek understanding of assumptions, perceptions and interpretations.

Low _____/_____/_____/_____ High

Placing ideas on the table and pulling them off / placing data and perceptions before the group

1. We state the intentions of our communications.

Low _____/_____/_____/_____ High

2. We provide relevant facts, ideas, opinions and inferences.

Low _____/_____/_____/_____ High

3. We remove or announce modification of ideas, opinions and points of view.

Low _____/_____/_____/_____ High

Paying attention to self and others to monitor our ways of working

1. We balance participation and open opportunities for each other to contribute and respond.

Low _____/_____/_____/_____ High

2. We restrain our impulses to react, respond or rebut at inappropriate times or in ineffective ways.

Low _____/_____/_____/_____ High

3. We maintain awareness of the group's task, processes and development.

Low _____/_____/_____/_____ High

Presuming positive intentions to support a nonjudgmental atmosphere

1. We communicate respectfully whether we agree or disagree.

Low _____/_____/_____/_____ High

2. We embed positive presuppositions in our paraphrases, summaries and comments.

Low _____/_____/_____/_____ High

3. We embed positive presuppositions when we inquire or probe for specificity.

The Adaptive School: Developing and Facilitating Collaborative Groups . Center for Adaptive Schools . www.adaptive-schools.com

109

Personal Seven Norms Assessment

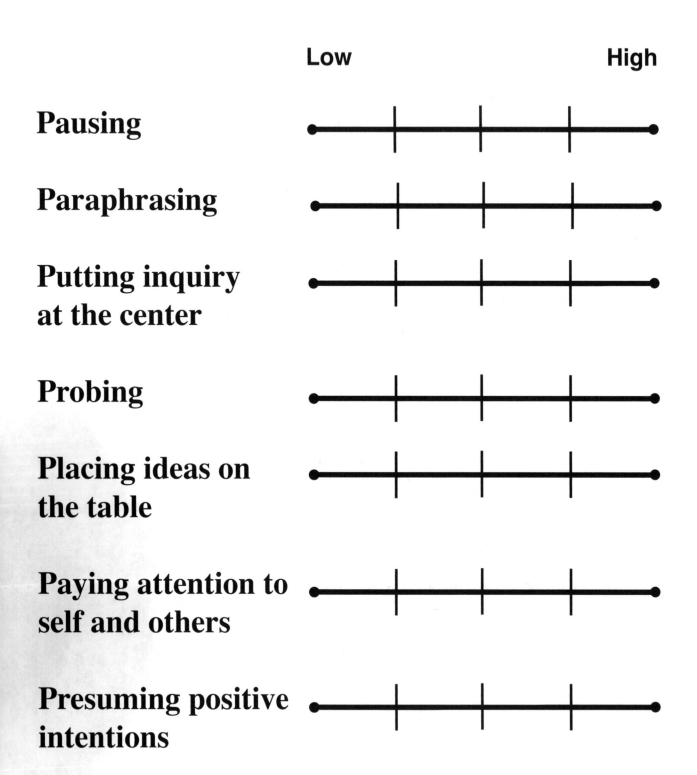

Low   High

Pausing

Paraphrasing

Putting inquiry
at the center

Probing

Placing ideas on
the table

Paying attention to
self and others

Presuming positive
intentions

The Adaptive School: Developing and Facilitating Collaborative Groups . Center for Adaptive Schools . www.adaptive-schools.com

110

Group Seven Norms Assessment

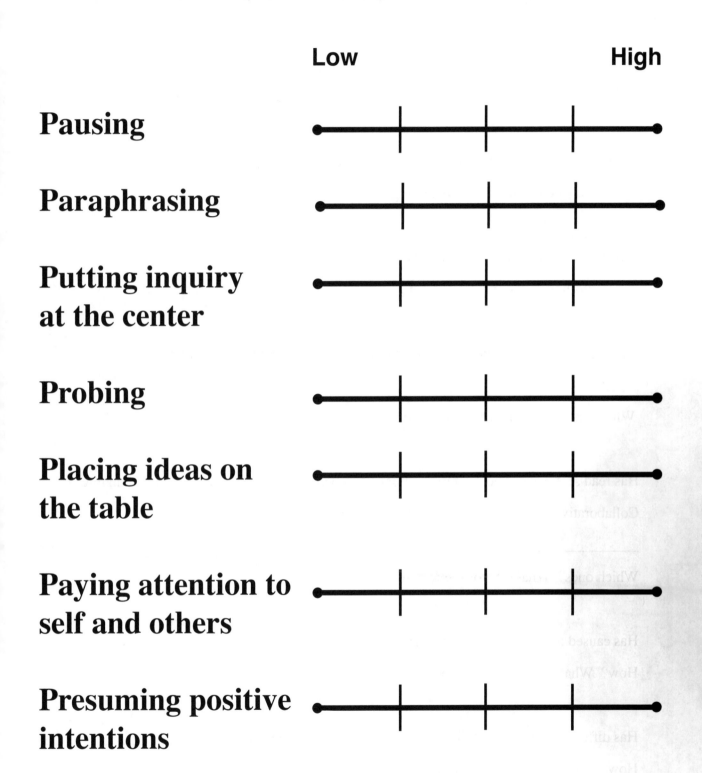

The Adaptive School: Developing and Facilitating Collaborative Groups . Center for Adaptive Schools . www.adaptive-schools.com

111

Adaptive Schools People Search

Directions: Find 9 people, each of whom can sign one line.

(No more than one person per line!) Obtain as many signatures as you can.

Has explained the Adaptive Schools work to others _____

      To whom? When? How did it go?

Has used a strategy from the Adaptive Schools _____

      With what group? How did it go?

Has improved on his or her use of one or more of the norms of collaboration

_____

 Which one(s)? What is he or she learning?

Has read sections of The Adaptive School: A Sourcebook for Developing and Facilitating

Collaborative Groups by Robert Garmston and Bruce Wellman

_____

Which ones? What is he or she learning?

Has caused a positive change in a meeting _____

How? What is he or she learning?

Has differentiated between dialogue and discussion with a group _____

How did it go? What is s/he learning?

The Adaptive School: Developing and Facilitating Collaborative Groups . Center for Adaptive Schools . www.adaptive-schools.com

112

Moving Forward

1. Adopt the five meeting standards

2. Rotate the facilitator and recorder roles

3. Select one or two norms to develop

4. Decide what is nonnegotiable

5. Teach topics groups should know

6. Provide space tools and time

7. Lighten up
   Laugh lots
   Listen well
   Locate power inside the group

The Adaptive School: Developing and Facilitating Collaborative Groups . Center for Adaptive Schools . www.adaptive-schools.com

113

Clock Partners

Make an appointment with four different people—one for each indicated hour on the clock. Be sure you each record the appointment on your clocks in the corresponding slot.

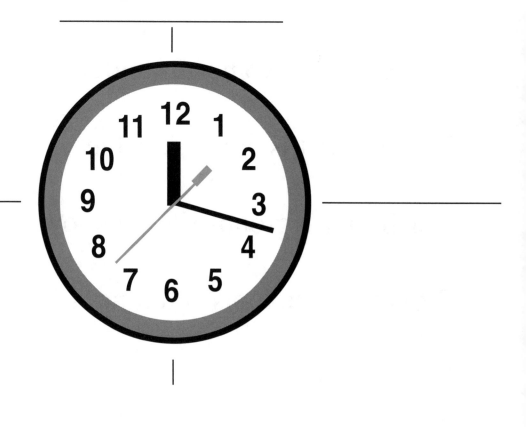

The Adaptive School: Developing and Facilitating Collaborative Groups . Center for Adaptive Schools . www.adaptive-schools.com

114

Fractal Partners

Make an appointment with four different people --- one for each slot. Be sure you each record the appoinment on your page in the corresponding slot.

_____

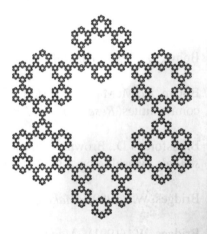

_____

The Adaptive School: Developing and Facilitating Collaborative Groups . Center for Adaptive Schools . www.adaptive-schools.com

115

Resources

Amason, A.C., Thompson, K.R., Hochwarter, W.A., & Harrison, A.W. (1995, Autumn) Conflict: An important dimension in successful management teams. *Organizational Dynamics*, 24 (2), 20-35.

Baker, W., Costa, A., & Shalit, S. (1997). The norms of collaboration: Attaining communicative competence. In A.L. Costa & R.M. Liebmann (Eds.), *The process-centered school: Sustaining a renaissance community.* (pp. 119-142) Thousand Oaks, CA: Corwin Press.

Bandura, A. (1977). *Selfefficacy: The exercise of control.* New York: W.H. Freeman.

Barbe, W. and Swassing, R. (1979). *Teaching through modality strengths: Concepts and practices.* Columbus, OH: Zaner-Bloser.

Barth, R. (1990). *Improving schools from within: Teachers, parents, and principals can make the difference.* San Francisco: Jossey-Bass.

Bacharach, S., and Mundell, B. (1995). *Images of schools: Structures and roles in Organizational behavior.* Thousand Oaks, CA: Corwin.

Block, P. (1981). *Flawless consulting: A guide to getting your expertise used.* Austin, TX: Learning Concepts.

Bohm, D. (1990). *On dialogue.* Ojai, CA: David Bohm Seminars.

Bolam, R., McMahon, A., Stoll, L., Thomas, S., & Wallace, M. (2005). Creating and sustaining effective learning communitites. *Research brief RB637*, London: DfES Publications. www.dfes.gov.uk/research/.

Bransford, J.D., Brown, A.L., and Cocking, R.R. (1999). *How people learning: Brain, mind, experience, and schools.* Washington, DC: National Academy Press.

Bridges, W. (1980). *Making sense of life's changes: Transitions.* Reading, MA: Addison-Wesley

Bridges, W. (1991). *Managing transitions, making the most of changes.* Reading, MA: Addison-Wesley

Briggs, J, and Peat, D. (1999). *Seven life lessons of chaos.* New York: HarperCollins.

Bryk, A., & Schneider, B. (2002). *Trust in schools: A core resource for improvement.* New York: The Russell Sage Foundation.

Buckley, M. Visual Voyages, 3 Lost Acre Trail, Sherman, CT 06784-2627, Phone: (860) 354-4543, Fax: (860) 354-6740, EMail; Micbuck@aol.com.

Capra, Fritjof. (1991). *The tao of physics.* Boston: Shambala..

Center for Conflict Resolution. (1978). *A manual for group facilitators.* Madison, WI: Center for Conflict Resolution.

The Adaptive School: Developing and Facilitating Collaborative Groups . Center for Adaptive Schools . www.adaptive-schools.com

116

Resources

Center for Conflict Resolution. (1981). *Building united judgment: A handbook for consensus decision making*. Madison, WI: Center for Conflict Resolution.

Collins, J.C. & Porras, J.I. (1997). *Built to last: Successful habits of visionary companies*. New York: HarperBusiness. 43-45.

Chatwin, B. (1987). *The Songlines*. New York: Penguin.

Costa, A. and Garmston, R. (2002). *Cognitive coaching: A foundation for renaissance schools*. Norwood, MA: Christopher-Gordon..

Covey, S.. (1989). *The 7 habits of highly effective people*. New York: Fireside.

Crum, T. (1987). *The magic of conflict*. New York: Touchstone.

Donohue, W. and Kolt, R.. (1992). Managing interpersonal conflict. Newbury Park, CA: Sage.

Doyle, M. and Straus, D. (1993). *How to make meetings work*, New York: Berkley.

Drucker, P. (1993). *Post-capitalist society*. New York: HarperBusiness.

Dufour, R., Eaker, R., & Baker, R. (1998). *Professional learning communities at work: Best practices for enhancing student achievement*. Bloomington, IN: National Educational Services.

Elgin, S.H. (1980). *The gentle art of verbal self-defense*. New York: Dorset.

Elmore, R. (1995 December). Structural Reform and Educational Practice. *Educational research,* Vol. 24, No. 9, pp. 23-26.

Elmore, R. (2000). *Building a new structure for school leadership*. The Albert Shanker Institute. Winter 2000.

Fisher, R., Kopelman, E. and Schneider, A. (1994). *Beyond machiavelli: Tools for coping with conflict*. Cambridge, MA: Harvard University Press.

Fullan, M. (2001). The new meaning of educational change (3rd ed.). New York: Teachers College Press.

Garmston, R. & Wellman, B. (1992). *How to make presentations that teach and transform*. Alexandria VA: Association for Supervision and Curriculum Development.

Garmston, R. & Wellman, B. (1998). Teacher talk that makes a difference. *Educational Leadership,* 55 (7), 30-34.

Garmston, R. (2005). *The presenter's fieldbook: A practical guide*. Norwood, MA: Christopher-Gordon.

The Adaptive School: Developing and Facilitating Collaborative Groups . Center for Adaptive Schools . www.adaptive-schools.com

117

Resources

Garmston, Robert and Wellman, Bruce. (2009). *The adaptive school: A sourcebook for developing collaborative groups.* Norwood, MA: Christopher-Gordon.

Garmston, Robert and Wellman, Bruce. (1995, April). Adaptive Schools in a Quantum Universe. *Educational Leadership,* Vol. 52, No. 7, pp. 6-12.

Gell-Mann, Murray. (1994). *The quark and the jaguar: Adventures in the simple and the complex,* New York: W.H. Freeman

Gerstein, Arnold and Reagan, James. (1986). *Win-win approaches to conflict resolution.* Salt Lake City: Peregrine Smith.

Gleick, J. (1987). Chaos: Making a new science. New York: Viking Penguin.

Glickman, Carl D. (1993). *Renewing America's schools, A guide for school-based action.* San Francisco: Jossey-Bass .

Goddard, R., Hoy, W., & Woolfolk Hoy, A. (2004). Collective efficacy beliefs: Theoretical developments, empirical evidence, and future directions. *Educational Researcher*, Vol. 33, (3), 3-13.

Goleman, Daniel. (1995). *Emotional intelligence: Why it can matter more than IQ.* New York: Bantam.

Goleman, D. (2006). *Social intelligence: The revolutionary new science of human relations. New York: Bantam Dell.*

Grinder, M. (1997). *The science of nonverbal communications.* Battleground, WA: Michael Grinder and Associates.

Grinder, M. (2007). *The elusive obvious: The science of non-verbal communication.* Battle Ground, WA: Michael Grinder and Associates.

Haeckel, Stephan. (1999). *Adaptive Enterprise.* Boston: Harvard Business School Press.

Hoy, W., Tarter, J., & Woolfolk Hoy, A.. (2006). Academic Optimism of schools: A force for student achievement. *American Educational Research Journal*, 43, (3), 425-446.

Jaques, J. & Cason, K. (1994). *Human capability: A study of individual potential and its applications.* Falls Church, VA: Cason & Hall.

Johnson, B. (1996). *Polarity management: Identifying and managing unsolvable problems.* Amherst, MA: HRD Press.

Kegan, R., & Lahey, L. (1984). Adult leadership and adult development: A constructivist view. In B. Kellerman (Ed.), *Handbook on socialization theory and research* (pp. 199–229). Chicago: Rand McNally.

Kegan, R., & Lahey. L. (2001). *How the way we talk can change the way we work: Seven languages of transformation.* San Francisco: Jossey-Bass.

The Adaptive School: Developing and Facilitating Collaborative Groups . Center for Adaptive Schools . www.adaptive-schools.com

118

Resources

LaBorde, G.Z. (1984). *Influencing with integrity: Management skills for communication and negotiation*. Palo Alto, CA: Syntony, 163.

Leatherman, D. (1990). *The training trilogy, facilitation skills*. Amherst, MA: Human Resource Development Press.

Lee, V., & Smith, J. (1996). Collective responsibility for learning and its effects on gains in achievement and engagement for early secondary students. *American Journal of Education*, 104, 103–147.

Lewin,R. (1992). *Complexity, life at the edge of chaos*. New York: Macmillan Publishing Co.

Lipton. L., & Wellman, B. (1998). *Pathways to understanding: Patterns and practices in the learning-focused classroom*. Sherman, CT: MiraVia.

Little, J. W. (1982). Norms of collegiality and experimentation: Workplace conditions of school success. *American Educational Research Journal*, 19, 225-340.

Little, J. W. (1990). The persistence of privacy: Autonomy and initiative in teachers' professional relations. *Teachers College Record*, 91, 509-536.

Little, J., & McLaughlin, M. (Eds.). (1993). *Teachers' work: Individuals, colleagues, and contexts*. New York: Teachers College Press.

Lortie, D. (1975). *Schoolteacher: A sociological study*. Chicago: University of Chicago Press.

Louis, K. & Kruse, S. (1995). *Professionalism and community: Perspectives on reforming urban schools*. Thousand Oaks, CA: Corwin Press.

Louis, K. S., Marks, H. M., & Kruse, S. (1996). Teachers' professional community in restructuring schools. *American Educational Research Journal*, 33 (4), 757-798.

Markova, D. (1992). *The Art of the Possible: A Compassionate Approach to Understanding The Way People Think, Learn and Communicate*. Emeryville, CA: Conari.

Margulies, Nancy. (1991). *Mapping inner space: Learning and teaching mind mapping*. Tucson, AZ: Zephyr.

McLaughlin, M., & Talbert, J. (2001). *Professional communities and the work of high school teaching*. Chicago: University of Chicago Press.

McLaughlin, M., & Talbert, J. (2006). *Building school-based teacher learning communities: Professional strategies to improve student achievement*. New York: Teachers College Press.

Mindell, A. (1992). *The leader as martial artist: Techniques and strategies for resolving conflict and creating community*. San Francisco: Harper.

Morgan, G. (1986). *Images of organization*. New York: Sage.

The Adaptive School: Developing and Facilitating Collaborative Groups . Center for Adaptive Schools . www.adaptive-schools.com

119

Resources

Newman, F. and Associates. (1997). *Authentic Achievement*. San Francisco: Jossey-Bass.

Perkins, David. (1992). *Smart Schools*. New York: Free Press.

Project Star: A Private Universe. (1992). Video by Pyramid Film and Video, 2801 Colorado Avenue, Santa Monica, CA 90404, (310) 828-7577.

Pruitt, D. & Carnevale, P. (1993). *Negotiation in social conflict*. Pacific Grove, CA: Brooks/Cole.

Rosenholtz, S. (1991). *Teachers' workplace: The social organization of schools*. New York: Teachers College Press.

Rowe, M. B. (1986, January-February). Wait time: Slowing down may be a way of speeding up! *Journal of Teacher Education.*, 43–49.

Sanders, W., & Rivers, J. (1996). *Cumulative and residual effects of teachers on future student academic achievement*. Knoxville, TN: Universtity of Tennessee Value-Added Research and Assessment Center.

Saphier, J., Bigda-Peyton, T., & Pierson, G. (1989). *How to make decisions that stay made*. Alexandria, VA: Association for Supervision and Curriculum Development.

Saphier, J., Haley-Speca, M., & Gower, R. (2008). *The skillful teacher: Building your teaching skills*. Acton, MA: Research for Better Teaching.

Sarason, S. (1990). *The predictable failure of educational reform*. San Francisco: Jossey-Bass.

Schein, E. (2004). *Organizational culture and leadership (3rd ed.)*. San Francisco: Jossey-Bass.

Schwartz, R. (2002). *The skilled facilitator: Practical wisdom for developing effective groups*. San Francisco: Jossey-Bass.

Schein, Edgar H. (1993, Autumn). On Dialogue, Culture and Organizational Learning. *Organizational Dynamics*. New York: American Management Association. pp. 40-51.

Schmuck, Richard A. and Runkel, Philip J. (1994). *The Handbook of Organization Development in Schools and Colleges*. Fourth Edition. Prospect Heights, IL: Waveland Press, Inc.

Schwartz. Peter. (1991). *The art of the long view: Planning for the future in an uncertain world*. New York: Doubleday Currency.

Schwartz, R. (2002). *The skilled facilitator: Practical wisdom for developing effective groups*. San Francisco: Jossey-Bass.

Senge, P. M. (1990). *The fifth discipline: The art and practice of the learning organization*. New York: Doubleday/Currency.

Senge, Peter M, et. al. (1994). *The fifth discipline fieldbook*. New York: Doubleday.

The Adaptive School: Developing and Facilitating Collaborative Groups . Center for Adaptive Schools . www.adaptive-schools.com

120

Resources

Senge, Peter M., et al. (1999). *The dance of change: The challenges to sustaining momentum in learning organizations*, New York: Doubleday.

Sergiovanni, T. (1994). *Building community in schools*. San Francisco: Jossey-Bass.

Stacey, R. (1992). *Managing the unknowable: Strategic boundaries between order and chaos in organizations*. San Francisco: Jossey-Bass. 13.

Sylwester, Robert. (1995). *A celebration of neurons: An educator's guide to the human brain*. Alexandria, VA: ASCD.

Timer Tools®. www.kaganonline.com. 800-933-2667

Thomas, Stephen D. (1987). *The last navigator*. New York: Ballantine.

Tschannen-Moran, M., Woolfolk-Hoy, A.W., & Hoy, W. (1998). Teacher efficacy: Its meaning and measure. *Review of Educational Research*, 68, 202-248.

Tyack, D., & Cuban, L. (1995). *Tinkering toward utopia. A century of public school reform*. Cambridge, MA: Harvard University Press.

Ury, W. (1991). *Getting past no: Negotiating your way from confontation to cooperation*. New York: Bantam

Wagner, Tony. (1994). *How schools change: Lessons from three communities*. Boston: Beacon.

Waldrop, M. (1992). *Compleixity: The emerging science at the edge of order and chaos*. New York: Simon and Schuster

Waters, T., & Grubb, S. (2004). *Leading schools: Distinguishing the essential from the important*. Aurora, CO: Mid-Continent Research for Education and Learning.

Wellman, B., & Lipton, L. (2004). *Data-driven dialogue: A facilitator's guide to collaborative inquiry*. Sherman, CT: MiraVia.

Wheatley, M. (1992). *Leadership and the new science: Learning about organizations from and orderly universe*. San Francisco: Barrett-Koehler.

The Adaptive School: Developing and Facilitating Collaborative Groups . Center for Adaptive Schools . www.adaptive-schools.com

121

Notes

The Adaptive School: Developing and Facilitating Collaborative Groups . Center for Adaptive Schools . www.adaptive-schools.com

122

Notes

The Adaptive School: Developing and Facilitating Collaborative Groups . Center for Adaptive Schools . www.adaptive-schools.com

123

Notes

The Adaptive School: Developing and Facilitating Collaborative Groups . Center for Adaptive Schools . www.adaptive-schools.com

124

For Information About Seminars

Call for consultation on designing made-to-order workshops and seminars for your group. Associates at The Center for Adaptive Schools have extensive experience working with district leadership teams, elementary, middle and high school faculties, intermediate agencies and other groups. We provide workshops in each of four leadership hats: presenting, consulting, coaching, and facilitating. We will be happy to talk with you about your plans or help you design specific services to meet your needs.

For information please check our website:
www.adaptiveschools.com   **or contact:**

Lisa Joseph
Center for Adaptive Schools
P.O. Box 630128
Highlands Ranch CO 80163
303-683-6146 Voice
303-791-1772 Fax

Order Additional Copies
For councils, colleagues and faculties

The Adaptive School: Developing and Facilitating Collaborative Groups (Syllabus)
(2009) Garmston, R. and Wellman, B. (note: special rates are available for bulk purchases)

The Adaptive School: A Sourcebook for Developing Collaborative Groups
(2009) Garmston, R. and Wellman, B. (note: special rates are available for bulk purchases)

Order Related Titles

Cognitive Coaching: A Foundation for Renaissance Schools Second Edition
(2002) Costa, A. and Garmston, R

(note: special rates are available for bulk purchases when working with the Center for Cognitive Coaching - www.cognitivecoaching.com)

The Presenter's Field Book: A Practical Guide (2005) Garmston, R.

Christopher-Gordon Publishers, Inc.
1420 Providence Highway, Suite #120
Norwood, MA 02062
Phone: (800) 934-8322 or (781) 762-5577
Fax: (781) 762-2110

The Adaptive School: Developing and Facilitating Collaborative Groups . Center for Adaptive Schools . www.adaptive-schools.com

125